Changing Patterns
of
Human Behavior

An Introduction
to
The Structural Pattern Reframing

Jan Dyba, M. A.

Structural Human Science Publishing & Jan Dyba Research Group

Copyediting by Monika Chorąży
Cover image by Mirosław Nadymus

To Daria

The creative spirit of Milton H. Erickson
and Ernest L. Rossi, whose great work inspired me to do my own

CONTENTS

old pattern/The introductory work with perspective/Utilizing the patient's resources/The creation of a new frame of reference/The establishment of the departure from the old pattern of behavior

INTRODUCTION

Psychotherapy may be defined in various ways. In general, we can assume that it is an art of creating a change in the behavior or at the levels of cognitions and emotions. This change is supposed to head towards the direction of better health or state of well-being of the patient. Depending on a patient, their problems and the therapeutic modality, the length of the treatment can vary. From time to time, however, in the field of psychotherapy, an individual emerges who is able to achieve better and more permanent results in short periods of time, and very often in some strange, unknown way. Many times those people start some new currents of thought in psychotherapy. Not many, however, are able to replicate the results achieved by such people, even after a long training. On many occasions, the author talked about this phenomenon with others and they came up with a straight conclusion. All these incredible individuals had some kind of special features, intuitions, personal traits that enabled them to work in their unique way.

The book, the reader is holding in hands now, tries to look at that kind of people from a different perspective - the perspective of
a learning process. When we look at geniuses in any filed we see them at their fifties, sixties or seventies. They all have life of experience behind them. In the process of learning any skill there is a period when we learn consciously. In a process of learning how to drive a car, we learn how to use accelerator and clutch together in synchrony. At first, we put a lot of attention into it. At this point any other thing distracts us from the main task. Radio, talking or anything else distracts and stresses us. After some time, we are able to drive the car and do many other things at the same time. The ability of driving a car became automatic. Automatic skills are, in their nature, semi-unconscious. Take, for example, the ability to work on the computer. How many times did it happen to you that someone called and asked you about how to do something with Word or Excel? And how many times, if it happened, you were unable to tell right away? Many times people have to sit in front of a computer and just do it to recall it. How many times are we just doing things and are unable to explain step by step how we are doing it? It happens this way due to the processes of automation. The theoretical part of the knowledge becomes, in part, inaccessible to us on the conscious level. The same process occurs in every field of knowledge when we are dealing with the process of increasing expertise. The main thesis of this book is that maybe we are dealing with the same process also in the field of psychotherapy, and due to this, some parts of the unique approaches of the great therapists are lost in the process of conceptualization of their way of work.

The models and ideas presented here are a result of a six year long project that was dedicated to finding the structure which stands behind therapeutic genius of such unique personalities as described above. Three unique therapists were chosen as subjects for analysis: Milton H. Erickson, Anthony Robbins and Byron Katie. The author selected to the main analysis only the psychotherapeutic processes that took one to two sessions to be able to seize the whole process of change. Next, the selected sessions were analyzed in two ways. One was to look for similarities in few different sessions of single therapist, and another was to look for the similarities between the sessions of different therapists.

The following book presents the model that seizes the key points similar to all these three therapists. It, therefore, does not demonstrate a model of work of any of these three, it shows something different - something that none of them does as presented here, but something that parts of the readers can find in the way of working with patients in all three of them.

This book does not present techniques of work but rather tries to describe the technology standing behind the techniques.

How to read this book

The first part of the book presents the main concepts that are required to get acquainted with understanding the whole model of intervention. Therefore, it is advised to spend some time on investigation of this part of the book.

The second part is dedicated to the detailed description of the model itself. It is divided into five chapters, each for one stage of the intervention. These chapters are constructed in such a way to enable a reader to investigate them separately. Due to this fact, a reader may find some basic ideas from the previous chapters repeated in part in an altered context in purpose to demonstrate the flow of some processes from one stage of the intervention to another. It also creates five separate parts, which makes it possible to study them separately. The author advises to study each part one at a time and then go through all of them one more time to enable the processes of integration of the whole model to take place.

PART ONE

PART ONE

In this part of the book we will address few general concepts that will enable us to understand the basics of the whole approach. It is important to go through it focused, for the purpose of creation of the ground on which all the more advanced action will take place.

1

THE CONCEPT OF A PATTERN OF BEHAVIOR

Before we start to go deeper into the theory and the Structural Pattern Reframing Model, we need to define the basic unit of analysis first. The basic unit of analysis is something that the therapist is looking for, it is part of a "glass" through which a therapist looks at the patient. And so, in different schools of psychotherapy, the therapists are dealing with different kinds of problems, and focus their attention on different things in the story the patient tells them. For example, in classical Freudian Psychoanalysis, the therapist deals mainly with the content suppressed to the unconsciousness. Almost the whole process of healing or change is based on the idea that the patient needs to get his suppressed memories back from the unconscious to the conscious mind. If this happens, suddenly the insight occurs, which is probably some kind of change in the meaning, and the resolution from the symptom follows that process (Freud, 1937, 1977). On the other side of therapeutic world, so called Radical Behaviorism puts as a basic unit of analysis a sample of behavior. A behavior is in this paradigm an observable action, a response to stimuli. In consequence, the behaviorists will focus purely on behavior and its change through the predesigned systems of reinforcements (Skinner, 1976; Watson, 1919, 1930). The Cognitive Behavioral Approaches add to the behavioral approach the cognitions. A person creates cognitions and acts upon them, feels certain things because of them and so on. The therapist identifies, for example, in case of Cognitive Behavioral Therapy, the automatic thoughts and alters them. In consequence the behavior alters (Beck, Emery, & Greenberg, 1985; Beck, Rush, Shaw, & Emery, 1979; Maultsby, 1984).

All the description above is certainly a great oversimplification and does not reflect even a tiny bit of what all these paradigms bring with them to the field of psychotherapy. The goal of this short introduction is not, however, a good detailed reconstruction of the above described schools. It is rather to prove a point that each and every school of psychotherapy brings with it some kind of basic assumptions among which there is always some basic unit the therapists are looking for and based on which they are working with the patient to achieve some results.

In the Structural Pattern Reframing Model that basic unit is a pattern of behavior. Now it may sound a bit similar to a behavioral standpoint where the basic unit is a simple observable behavior. The idea of a pattern of behavior is in general, a totally different concept.

The pattern of behavior is a kind of a set or a class of many behaviors that all work in favor of some goal or need. In fact, the unifying principle for a pattern of behavior is a goal or need underlying it. In strictly behavioral problems like, for example, phobias (Beck et al., 1985), these patterns may be quite simple and these will be composed of avoidance behaviors, emotional reactions while within close range from the subject of phobia, and some cognitions. One can as well include in it some ways of speaking about the phobia and subjects connected with it, for example, in other words the language that will reflect the pattern on a communication level. All this is a pattern of behavior. That kind of pattern can be then divided into smaller parts, a kind of subpatterns, like, for example, the cognitive pattern will include thoughts, emotional will include all emotional reactions, these two would be connected with a physiological subpattern and so on. The important thing here is that all these behaviors are directed towards the avoidance of a subject of the phobia. So there is a unifying principle for all of them, a need or a goal, that connects them somehow.

A depression is another, more complicated pattern. There are a lot of ways for depressive expression. It can, for example, express itself through special patterns of thoughts (Beck et al., 1979), as well as behaviors like, for example, lack of appetite or sleep disorders, as well as general lower or sad "depressive" mood, lack of force to do anything and so on. It is complicated because it manifests itself in many ways on many levels in life. It can manifest in language, for example, or in a general negativistic attitude (American Psychiatric Association, 1994). The depression may also, however, be a pattern of behavior leading to many different goals or satisfying many needs. For example, a person being in a depressive state will probably receive a lot of care from others, so we can identify the needs like: safety, comfort and so on, that would retain the pattern in place. On the other side, a person with a depression may also have many possibilities of punishing others, those who care, with a depressive set of behaviors. Many times that kind of behaviors may evoke feelings of guilt within the family members. This is, however, much more complicated topic, and we will not address it here. The important thing for us is to know that a pattern of behavior is complicated when it satisfies more than one need. It is also complicated when there is a huge set of behaviors in it, but it is the need that makes it really complicated. The therapist should remember the crucial role of identifying the needs standing behind the patterns. If well identified, one can expect the change process to occur, when, on the other hand, some needs or goals would be omitted, one can expect that, when this goals will not be met in a new patterns of behavior, the old ways of dealing with this situations will come back, and the old patterns will appear again.

Now, we can proceed further into the concept of the pattern and try to answer the question, what the pattern should look like? What are the definitional features of the pattern of behavior? Since in Structural Pattern Reframing the therapist uses the pattern as a main concept, they build around it a great part of the therapeutic reality. So it is a question about the definition of the patient's problem. This question will be also addressed in the part of this book dedicated to the description of the first phase of the General Model of Structural Pattern Reframing Intervention.

In general, we can outline few features that a well defined pattern of behavior should have. It has to have a need standing behind its specification. The pattern should also have a beginning and the end easily identifiable as well as it has to include some kind of process in it, some content.

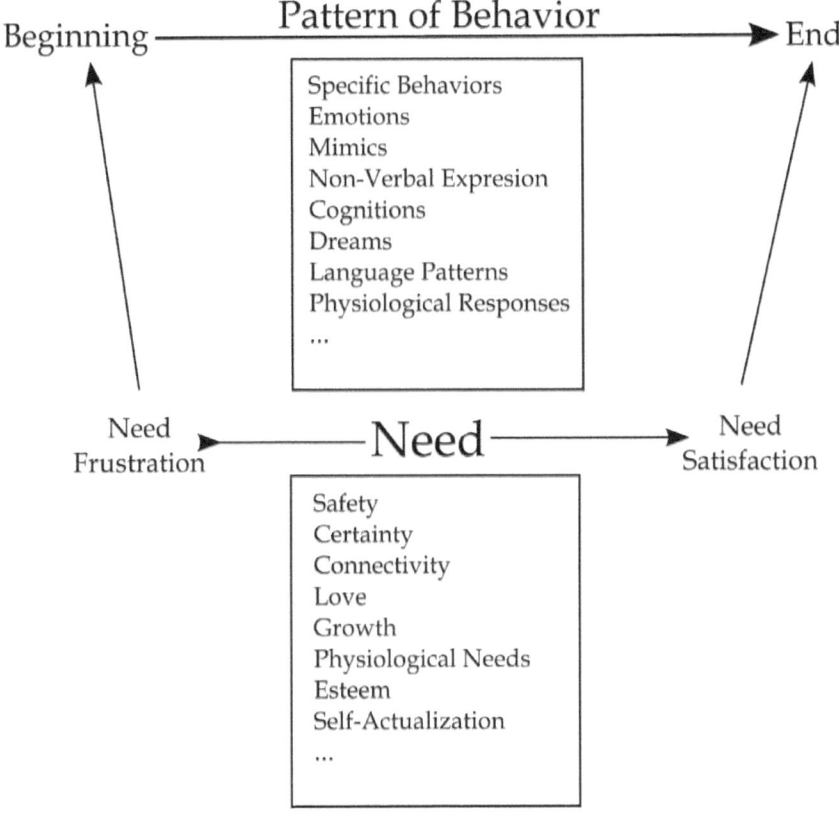

Figure 1. The structure of a problem situation or a pattern of behavior. The pattern of behavior is illustrated here with its beginning and end points as well as the content of it. The beginning of the pattern is correlated with a moment in time, where a frustration of a need of some kind occurs. Then the pattern triggers some specific behaviors, which leads to the need satisfaction and the end of the pattern sequence.

The author already discussed the importance of the identification of needs standing behind the pattern of behavior. The need or set of needs are the core feature of the pattern. It is because of the need that satisfies the patient, that they display a set of behaviors within the pattern. One of the first questions that a therapist should ask themselves when listening to the description of a patient's problem should be: what is the need standing behind this way of acting? What is the goal for it? In other words: why does a person do what they do?

To identify the needs or goals standing behind some actions one can use their own intuition or follow some ready-made schemas. The author will present here two widely known and very helpful schemas of human needs that may help people identify the needs standing behind the patterns of their own and others behavior.

First one is the Six Human Needs model created and applied by Anthony Robbins in his work (Robbins, 2007). Anthony Robbins concludes that people's actions may be referred to six human needs. First is a need for certainty, the one which gives us sense of safety and comfort. Second, the need for uncertainty, that is a need to experience change in life, so that it could be funny and exciting. This need of variety in life protects us from being bored with our own life. Another need is significance. It is a need that makes all the people want to feel more special, more unique. Many times this need pushes us to work harder, to achieve some goals, but also it stands behind many controversial behaviors and things we do to ourselves to feel unique. Another need is the need for love and connection. Robbins (2007) distinguishes between love and connection. Love in this taxonomy takes much more commitment, and if ends, can create a lot more hurt and disappointment but when lasts, it is much more rewarding. Some people would go into connection, because of the fear for commitment, due to some past experiences, for example. These four needs according to Anthony Robbins (2007) are met in some way by all the people in the world. One can meet these in a variety of ways, some are more adaptive and fulfilling, other may be even harmful, like, for example, addictions. Another two needs are, according to the author of this conception, connected to fulfillment. In this theory, a person cannot achieve fulfillment if the two needs below are not being met. The first one is a need for growth. It is the need for constant development and getting better and better in something. If a person does not develop themselves, they are in a state of stagnation according to Anthony Robbins (2007). The last need is a need to contribute beyond ourselves. Robbins (2007) clams that many activities are directed towards going beyond ourselves and change another people's lives, and that only then, a person can feel really fulfilled. So, in general, in this model we do have six needs matrix that can help us direct our ways of thinking towards specific details in the story of a patient.

Another useful motivation model is a classical theory of human motivation presented by Abraham Maslow first in the article "*A theory of human motivation*" published in the *Psychological Review* in 1943 (Maslov, 1943), and then developed within a book *Motivation and Personality* (Maslov, 2009). Maslow presents there the so called hierarchy or pyramid of human needs. These needs are basic factors that drive people activity and curiosity. The needs are gathered within a specific hierarchy in which the basic needs are at the bottom of the pyramid, and more complex, higher needs are higher, with the need for self-actualization at the top. The most basic set of needs that drives the behavior is a physiological set. These are purely the needs of the body. This set includes basic motivation for maintaining homeostasis, a kind of balance within a body. One satisfies these needs through eating, drinking, breathing, but also by sex and sleep, for example. Another set of needs is connected with safety. One can satisfy it by gathering goods, but also by having and maintaining a good job, for example. Problems with life stability or with Anthony Robbins need for certainty will all be affiliated with this need within the Maslov's model. Another is the need for love and belonging. It is due to this need that people last for close relationships, intimacy and so on. It is also the need that drives us towards the direction of having a family and friends. The same motivation will encourage us to become a part of some groups and associations. Forth set is affiliated with the esteem. All people achievements are affiliated with this need, as well as a need for being respected and admired by others. This need is strongly connected with our self-esteem and with the confidence we put into our own acts and ideas. The last set of needs is connected with the self-actualization. Self-actualization is the need within a person to develop and grow inside. It is kind of similar to Anthony Robbins' need for growth. This need reflects itself within a desire to achieve more and more within a domain of some sort. It is a desire of constant development.

Now, if we look closer into these two classifications, we can observe, that in many ways they are similar one to another. For example, Anthony Robbins' need for certainty is quite similar to the need for safety, and both of them reflect, in some way, a motivation to maintain a balance and comfort in life. Maslov's love and belonging is similar to Robbins' love and connection. Robbins' need for significance can be well reflected by the esteem set of needs that encourages people to be perceived as better than average, for example. By the same token, the needs for growth and contribution beyond ourselves are more or less the same as the need for self – actualization. The need for uncertainty in Robbins (2007) taxonomy does not have an equivalent in Maslovs theory, and the author of this book finds it particularly valuable in practice.

The theories described above outline some key basic motives that drives people to do and perform most of their actions. The point of this description in the following chapter of this book is, however, not to judge if these theories reflect the reality or not, but rather to provide a therapist with simple models of guidelines of what to look for in the reality of the client's problem. One can use the Robbins model (2007), or Maslov (1943, 2009) model of the needs to look for the needs that are satisfied by a particular pattern of behavior, and then, when one identifies these needs, they can think of ways to satisfy them in different directions. It is very important to remember, that we are not supposed to change the need standing behind the pattern hoping to change that behavior in this way, but rather we are supposed to find different ways of satisfying a particular need or set of needs in the course of a therapy. The reason for it is that the needs that we identify, are basic drives for human activities, and these cannot be changed into something else. The author met few therapists who claimed that needs or a whole system of needs of their patients had to be changed, however. Therefore, it is important to state one more time, that the therapist working within the Structural Pattern Reframing Model does not change the needs. They respect the needs of a person and create the change by enabling alternative ways of satisfaction.

One of the great implications of such an approach is that each behavior, or set of behaviors, has some side benefits, even disorders such as a depression or eating disorders in this viewpoint all have some benefits and good sides that the therapist has to identify. The satisfaction of a need, even if in a harmful way for a patient, is a strong benefit coming out of maladaptive behavior. So, in conclusion, one can say, that with the identification of the needs standing behind the pattern of behavior, the identification of the benefits that the patient has from performing such behaviors has to be performed.

The other important feature of the pattern is so that it should be well defined itself. The pattern itself is a concept that is supposed to help a patient structure the reality of the problem in a more clear and understandable way. This goal can only be achieved if the maladaptive pattern of behavior is correctly and clearly defined. So, aside from the obvious principle that it has to have a goal or need standing behind it, it has to have the beginning, the end and the process well defined. In fact, the pattern itself is a behavior or set of behaviors that in its structure has a purpose or, in other words, some need specified, starts somewhere, ends in some point and goes through some specified steps in-between.

The beginning of the pattern is when the whole set begins. Many times the set of behaviors starts in response to some triggering events in the environment. For example, a husband reacting in certain way on his wife's requests may trigger some pattern. For instance, if the wife feels that her husband ignores her, she may react with anger of frustration. Now, in any case, it does not matter really if she is right in what she thinks is true. To the therapist, at this moment, it is important to notice what triggers certain responses and what evokes the pattern itself. Then, in the process of the therapeutic intervention, one can use a lot of reframing techniques to reframe the meaning of these reactions, and this may help replace the pattern. First, however, we need to identify the beginning of the pattern well enough.

The end of the pattern of behavior is a place in time where the pattern stops or replays. It is the place where the need or a goal standing behind the pattern is satisfied. Of course, almost all this mechanism is of unconscious nature and a patient would not be able to directly identify it, therefore, it is the therapist who has to point this out in the course of treatment.

The process is a part of the pattern of behavior that happens between the beginning and the end of it. So in general, it is all what happens. All the behaviors that lead us from the beginning to the end, from frustration of some need to its satisfaction, are in the process. All the quarrels, arguments, fights, aggression, all symptoms, moods, passive states and so on, in general, all behaviors that lead from the beginning to the end.

The task for the therapist is, when they decide to work in a framework of the Structural Pattern Reframing, to put the problem in the context of a pattern of behavior in such a way that the patient could see the whole course of their behaviors. It means that they would have a clear understanding of when something starts, why it starts, and that they are aware of the needs standing behind the pattern; what they do to achieve the goals standing behind the pattern, which means, the patient is aware of the process and what the result is, which means how the pattern satisfies the need of achieving the goal. When there is a problem redefined in such a way, it is automatically defined in solvable terms. There always will be other ways of achieving the same goals or satisfying the same need. In consequence, such a definition of situation almost always increases the amount of possibilities of action in the client's repertoire of behaviors and makes it possible to introduce some new ways of dealing with their reality.

2

UTILIZATION APPROACH

Another very important thing about the content of this book is to understand that the models and ideas presented in here are not some kind of patterns that one has to strictly follow from the first to the last step. The models presented here, especially the model of Structural Pattern Reframing, is a kind of idea, an inspiration for the therapist to help them orient a therapy in some kind of direction.

That is why it is important for the proper implementation and understanding of the ideas presented below to study a short description of one of the most important concept in therapy nowadays, at least from the Structural Pattern Reframing point of view. This concept is the Utilization Approach. Some people will refer to it as the utilization technique or techniques, but it is not actually some kind of technique, but rather a way of looking at people, an attitude.

The Utilization Approach was at first introduce by Milton H.

Erickson in his article originally published in the year of 1959 (Erickson, 1980c). Therein, he describes it in the following way:

"In Techniques of Utilization the usual procedure is reversed to an initial acceptance of the patients' presenting behaviors and a ready cooperation by the operator, however, seemingly adverse the presenting behaviors may appear to be in the clinical situation."

In other words, the clinician accepts the patient's presented behavior or unique personality trends and then uses it (utilizes) in such a way to promote the change and to facilitate the therapeutic trance(Erickson & Rossi, 1979). Carol Lankton(C. H. Lankton, 1985) puts it in this way:

"How are symptoms (or other problems, personality orientations, etc.) paradoxically prescribed so that the client continues the problem in a new way, that carries with it an opportunity to learn new options for behavior and freedom from that which has been prescribed? How is the symptom utilized to accomplish freedom from the symptom?"

The author of this book advises to all the readers to implement into their therapeutic practice the attitude of utilization, otherwise, there exists a possibility of wrong understandings of the further content of the following publication. What does it mean? It simply means to accept all the presented behaviors at first, and then try to think in a way of " how can I use this behavior, symptom etc. to facilitate a change in a desired way?"

Now, to gain some deeper understanding of the general idea let us look at the first ever described case of the Utilization Application. The case was described by Jeffrey Zeig during the course of his first meeting with Doctor Erickson(Zeig, 1980a). He describes the meeting of Doctor Erickson with a patient in Worcester State Hospital in 1930. When Doctor Erickson met the patient he (the patient) was nervously winding a string around the bars of the window in his room. He was doing it, because he thought that the bars were too thick and needed to be reinforced, otherwise his enemies would get him . And so he was reinforcing them by winding the string around them. Erickson decided to help him, moreover, he found the cracks in the floor and advised to stuff them with paper. Then, he pointed out that there were other rooms in the hospital that also needed to be well protected, and so the patient was in some time able to walk around the hospital. Then, Erickson was expanding his range by pointing out at the guards, then at the military that protected the state and the country. After some time the patient was able to leave the hospital. The example shortly described above clearly demonstrates the idea standing behind the Utilization Approach. A therapist should look at the patient, accept the given reality and work within this reality gradually towards change. To do it, one has to look at the patient in a certain way, so we can say, that the utilization approach is a way of looking at the patient and a way of looking at their problems as resourceful behaviors.

What does it mean that the behavior is resourceful? We will be looking for the answer to that question in a moment, but first, let us start with another question. What can we utilize? In his book (Erickson & Rossi, 1979) Doctor Erickson describes following ideas:

1. Patients manifested behavior: Erickson presented many ways of utilizing the patients manifested behavior in favor to trance induction and its facilitation. For example (Erickson, 1980c) with a patient that was compulsively pacing the floor and could not just sit or lie quietly he said:

"Are you willing to cooperate with me *by continuing to pace the floor, even as you are doing now?*" The patient answered that either way he has to do it while in the office. Erickson was then participating in directing the patient into some directions. Finally, he started to direct the patient in various ways towards the chair on which he could sit and relax. Here are some examples:

"Now turn to the right away from the chair in which you can sit; turn left toward the chair in which you can sit; walk towards the chair in which you can sit (...) "the chair which *you will soon approach so to seat yourself comfortably.*" (...) the chair in which *you will shortly find yourself sitting comfortably.*"

Notice how Doctor Erickson slightly changes the way in which the directions are given, so that they have gradual suggestions implemented within (in italics added by the author of this book).

2. Emergency situations: According to Erickson (Erickson & Rossi, 1979) emergency situations are highly trance inductive. Therefore, some people may unwillingly present others with some kind of suggestions causing them to suffer in the future from, for example, psychosomatic problems. That is why one is supposed to be able to utilize such highly trance inductive situations in favor of positive change or resolution. The examples provided by Erickson are based on his children's experiences (Erickson & Rossi, 1979). In one case he focused his child attention on the color of the blood and the question, if it is red enough, so the child could redirect the attention from the pain experience. Then Erickson introduced a bit of competition into the situation by pointing out to the child that:

"his injury was not large enough to warrant as many stitches as his sister had at the time of her hand injury."

In the end the child lamented at the surgeon office that he would not have as many stitches as his sister, at the same time being totally unaware of the pain.

3. Patients inner realities: By inner realities Erickson meant the thoughts, feelings and experiences of the patients. The therapist may use patients' concepts of how the trance induction should look like to induce one. Therapist may also induce a trance by calling up on previous trance experiences.

4. Patients resistances: According to Erickson, a resistant behavior is an expression of patient individual self (Erickson & Rossi, 1979). Sometimes just accepting it and allowing it to express itself enables further work (Erickson, 1980c). On another occasion, one has to utilize the resistance to facilitate the trance. The therapist may do it by creating such a situation in which any response, even the resistance will be considered as cooperative reaction. It is good to remember that the resistance is an opposite reaction to the one the therapist asks about. One can use this tendency to evoke the behaviors they really desire. To do it, one has to create such a situation in which these reactions would be the opposite for these asked for.

5. Negative affects and confusion: Doubts, depressive states, fears and so on, may also be utilized to facilitate therapeutic trance and change. For example, when one doubts or fears to go into a trance, the therapist may use it and focus the attention on states and outer objects just

experienced, slowly narrowing and directing the attention inward.

6. Symptoms: Erickson, for example, describes an example of a patient that had to go through the dental treatment but was unable to develop the hypnotic anesthesia in the area of his mouth. He was able to develop the anesthesia in his hand very well but not in his mouth. In fact, the more the doctor tried to direct him toward the anesthesia in the region of his mouth, the more pain he felt down there. When he was brought over to Erickson, he developed the relaxation state and the suggestion was given so that, when he will be going through the dental treatment, he would develop the hyperesthesia, a painful experience in his hand. When he accomplished these suggestions, he spontaneously developed an anesthesia in his mouth at the same time.

Above, there is a classical view point on the matter of Utilization presented (Erickson & Rossi, 1979; Erickson, 1980c). Other interesting ideas can be found in the article of Jeffrey K. Zeig (Zeig, 1994) one of the closest students of Milton H. Erickson. In his article, Zeig also answers the question of what to utilize, and he presents the following ideas:

1. Sequences: The therapist may utilize sequences. A sequence is somehow similar to the pattern of behavior in the structural model presented in this book. It has a beginning, an end and some content. Doctor Zeig himself defines sequence as follows:

   "(...) a psychotherapy problem can be considered a sequence that begins with a trigger and proceeds through a series of behaviors, perceptions, internal dialogue, emotions, attitudes, relationship patterns, etc."

A Sequence can be utilized to facilitate the induction as well as therapeutic goals. Therapist may use sequence in variety of ways. They may use it to absorb patient, or they may reframe the sequence to outline the positive qualities of it, thus use it as a solution. Sequences neutral to the problem may also be used, for example, to facilitate trance experience.

2. Symptom words: Therapist may use the words in which patients describe their problems as "solution words". Therapist may positively reframe the meaning of these words, thus changing the meaning of the problem, or they may intersperse them into the induction, and use them to facilitate the positive trance experience.

3. Figures of speech: Symbols and proverbs inherited in cultural and language patterns may serve as a powerful resource for presenting ideas, suggestions or therapeutic goals to the patient. Therapist may use all the symbols from the culture that the patient comes from.

For further explanation on this model as well as case studies see Zeig (1994).

The ideas about the Utilization presented above illustrate in short what Doctor Erickson understood under this term. The main purpose of presenting this knowledge here is not to analyze and describe in detail the phenomena itself, but rather to signal to the reader the general attitude that will be helpful in understanding and applying the structures presented later in this book. For further readings and more detailed case studies the reader may direct his or her attention towards original Doctor Ericksons publications in this area (Erickson, Rossi, & Rossi, 1976; Erickson & Rossi, 1979; Erickson, 1980c).

What is a resource?

Now, as we already know a bit about what the Utilization Approach is, what can be a resource then? How do we define a resource? In this broader context of utilization, a resource can be anything, any thought, or any behavior, that one can utilize in the client's process of change. One can use the way a person speaks and uses language to facilitate some change, one can use the symptoms to achieve some therapeutic change, one can also utilize a resistance, and anything else. The question in case of resources is not whether something can be a resource or not. It is more the question if a therapist can see a potential in a behavior. It is a question of whether the therapist is able to find a way to use the behavior of a client, their attitude, their language patterns, mood patterns and so on, to facilitate a change.

The resource is, therefore, more an attitude derived from the Utilization Approach than some specific behavior. In general, anything can be utilized and, therefore, viewed as a resource in some context and way. It is at last the ability and a skill of the therapist to utilize that decides whether or not a behavior will be a resource or not in a given moment in time in a specific therapeutic situation.

In conclusion, we can assume that the resources are more a point of view, a perspective than specific behaviors. It is a specific perspective in which one is looking for the usefulness of the patient's behavior in a process of change. The Utilization Approach is in this perspective a way of using all this behaviors and symptoms manifested by the patient in such a way that they facilitate the process of change.

To summarize, it is of crucial value to get familiar with the idea of utilization and viewing a patient's problem behaviors as resources, or opportunities. Such an attitude will be of great importance to anyone who would like to reframe the pattern in a positive way and thus, enable different ways of satisfying the needs standing behind it.

PART TWO

PART TWO

This part of the book presents the General Model of Structural Intervention which is a core element of the whole Structural Pattern Reframing Model. One more time the author advises to go through every chapter separately and then read it one more time to be able to integrate it into a process.

3

THE GENERAL MODEL OF STRUCTURAL INTERVENTION

Through the years of education, research and training the author observed that a good therapist, or a person who works with people and achieve results, many times develops a unique way of working with others - their own way of looking at problems and dealing with them. Many times the consequence of such a new way is an approach that emerges some kind of new school of therapy or coaching. Often many details of a unique way of work of some therapist become uncovered or unnoticed. This part of the book presents an attempt to make some of the details more clear to the audience. The General Model of Structural Intervention is an attempt to take more than one great therapist and try to see what they have in common, and then to create from it a simple structure that will provide other people in the field with easy guidelines that would enrich their ways of work.

Earlier intervention models

Many times in the past people were asking a question of how to do a therapy. How should a general model or the treatment plan look like? At the beginning of this part of the book, we will address some earlier influential stage theories of the therapeutic process created in the past. Through this we will be able to get familiar with some different concepts and then see how much they have in common with the model presented in this book. The first psychotherapist noticing the stage nature of the therapeutic change was Carl Gustav Jung (Groesbeck, 1985; Howard, Lueger, Maling, & Martinovich, 1993). In his model he outlined four stages of psychotherapy: confession, elucidation, education, and "analysis proper", called elsewhere transformation. Confession starts the therapeutic process. During this stage patient rapports the problem to the therapist, which results in a relief. At this time, also a therapeutic relation is being created. At the second stage explanations are being given to the patient. It expands, in consequence, the patient's understandings of the problem. The period of education starts when we help the client to learn new patterns of behavior. It is the time when patient learns how to react differently in the situations and learns different ways of maintaining the problem. The last stage, transformation, does not focus so much on the behavior, but rather on the person as a whole. In this process the patient changes as a whole, through the special kind of relationship with the therapist. In fact, the relationship established during the process of psychotherapy changes both the patient and the therapist.

Another interesting example which influenced brief models of therapy was a sequential model proposed by Otto Fenichel (Fenichel, 1954) which describes therapeutic intervention in three sequential stages:

The first stage is a diagnosis which is a bit similar to the confession stage, and its main goal is to bring up possibly full spectrum of the problem; on the second stage the therapist chooses the proper treatment strategy and finally, in the third phase, the therapist applies this strategies together with the patient.

Ericksonian Models of Intervention

Before we will fall into the description of the General Model of Structural Intervention we need to address some ideas in the field of Ericksonian Approach on the same subject, due to the fact that it is the work of Milton H. Erickson that in major part influenced the Structural Model presented in this publication. We will shortly describe two models. First one, a newer provided by Ernest L. Rossi (Rossi, 1995) and another of great importance, because proposed by Milton H. Erickson himself (Erickson & Rossi, 1979).

Rossi (1995) in his book *The Psychobiology of Mind-Body Healing,* presents three stage general model of change.

The first stage provides the therapy with the time frames and initiates the so called inner search. By inner search we understand, in this context, a specific readiness of the unconscious mind to start a work for the benefit of the client towards the resolution of their problem. In this stage, the patient talks about the problem and in this process of expression some sort of basic restructuring happens. In other words, a lot of things happen when patient expresses the problem state outside, into the therapeutic situation. First of all, they can confront it with the therapist and their point of view, as well as gain a distance from the problem, so that it would not be so emotionally overwhelming. All this can influence and change the meaning of the problem. Rossi (Rossi, 1995) states that the basis of the restructuring process lies in the nature of memory processes themselves. Using the neurobiological data about creation of the memory traces, he claims (1995) that each time the memory of the problem is brought back from the memory, it is being actively constructed and not just brought back. In such a case, each recall of the memory is a different construction and so it changes through time. The end result of this stage is a creation of the positive therapeutic structure. This structure is some kind of readiness to follow the suggestion. The patient waits with hope for an answer from the therapist. In this stage, a shift from the linear rationale left hemisphere way of thinking and analysis into more archaic right hemispheric holistic and creative way of thinking takes place. That kind of thinking is more proper for the unconscious mind, and so stimulates the unconscious processes towards new understandings and solutions for the problem (Erickson & Rossi, 1979; Rossi, 1995; Watzlawick, 1978).

The second stage is approaching the state-depended resources. In this phase, the unconscious mind works towards the resolution of the problem. At the beginning of this process, a therapist allows the patient to just be in the altered state and let the unconscious work by using and combining the resources. These resources could be states, past memories, experiences and so on. Basically at this point, the unconsciousness does huge inner search during which it pulls out the state dependent resources and creates from it new understandings and solutions. State depended resources (Rossi, 1995) are these memories, associations, experiences and all other content which are attached to the certain state or mood or emotion, and can be retrieved from memory much more easily during the time a person is in a certain mood. During the process of hypnotic trance, which is a very specific state that includes hypnotic awareness and directed attention (Erickson, 1980b, 1980e), some special otherwise unavailable potential resources are available, as well as the ease within one can bring back states and memories increases, which makes it more easy to bring back any kind of resources for the unconscious work.

On a third stage, the therapist obtains some kind of confirmation from the unconsciousness about the problem resolution. One of the indicator of this process occurs when the patient spontaneously rapports his experiences in the altered state. When he refers to them as being in altered state, or in state of trans/hypnosis, in a state like on drugs, this means, that he was able to go deep enough to reach his inner state-depended resources and to modify and use them in a process of the problem solving (Rossi, 1995). One can also utilize some natural processes occurring during the hypnotic state to mark down this phase. For example, one could use the suggestions connected with going out of trance.

> When you feel that the work is done, you will slowly open your eyes and come back into the office.

The following is an example of much oversimplified suggestion but it illustrates the idea. Using similar but more built up suggestions the therapist attaches the observable phenomena like eyes opening and going out of the trance to the moment of inner search, when the problem is solved.

The Ernest L. Rossi (1995) model presented above assumes a kind of circularity in the therapeutic work. The model presents an idea of a therapeutic work in a framework of one of the currents in Ericksonian hypnotherapy. Rossi (1995) concludes that the following schema, when applied, will bring us to some kind of resolution for the problem sooner or later, but until it happens, it has to be slightly modified and repeated from session to session.

Milton H. Erickson – Three stage process

One of the most important models describing the process of psychotherapy for the development and understanding of Structural Pattern Reframing was proposed by Milton H. Erickson in his book *Hypnotherapy - an Exploratory Casebook* (Erickson & Rossi, 1979). Therein he presents together with Ernest L. Rossi a three stage process model describing his idea of a therapy and change.

The first stage of this model is the stage of preparation. During this stage, the therapist establishes a rapport or a therapeutic relation, develops the "yes set" or the acceptance of each other, and response attentiveness.

The therapist gathers the information about patients life experiences and symptoms that will be later utilized in a therapeutic trance. It is important to collect the information about the patient frame of reference in which they place the problem, as well. During this process Erickson claims it is "inevitable that new frames of reference and belief systems are created" (Erickson & Rossi, 1979, p. 2).

The second stage is the stage of therapeutic trance where the old habitual sets are temporary altered to allow the new, more constructive and changed promoting ones to be implemented. It is on this stage where the old framework is being depotentiated and the unconscious search through the personal associations and mental mechanisms begins. This leads to the hypnotic response, that is an expression of the behavioral potentials. In detail, that stage consists of the following substages.

First one is the fixation of attention. One can do it most effectively by recognizing and acknowledging the current experience of the patient. This, in consequence, leads to acceptance and develops the "yes set" – a some way automatic acceptation pattern for further suggestions.

Second stage consists of depotentiating habitual frameworks and belief systems. In this stage the therapist interrupts the patients habitual framework and the pattern of association. This interruption is also discussed by Ernest L. Rossi further as a creative moment (Rossi & Rossi, 2008; Rossi, 1972). Such a creative moment is a gap that emerges from the breaking of the habitual pattern of behavior. The new that emerges from such a break is a foundation of new insights and a change. According to Erickson (Erickson & Rossi, 1979), the best way to achieve such a state is by a surprise or a shock of some kind.

Unconscious search and unconscious process being the consequence of such an empty space described above, is another, third stage of the intervention. The unconscious search is initiated to look for some content to fill up the gap. This is a moment for some hypnotic suggestions to be introduced.

After this, the therapeutic response of some sort occurs during the trance, which is the manifestation of some of the behavioral potentials, expressed in an autonomous way.

The third stage of the general model is the ratification of the therapeutic change. On this stage, the patient has to, in a way, see for themselves that the change occurred. Some people are able to recognize it themselves and in some other cases the therapist must point it out in a way. The work and change that occurred have to be recognized, or it is highly possible that the old pattern will disrupt the still fragile and fresh new ways of reacting.

General Model of Structural Intervention

The General Model of Structural Intervention is in a way similar to the Ericksonian model of working with the patient in a therapeutic setting, but it also develops it and treats some parts of it in a more detailed way, making it more easy to implement into the daily practice. Below, the author presents a short overview of the whole model to provide the readers with a general framework. After this first introduction, each stage of the model will be described in detail to provide the reader with deeper understanding of the process of change standing behind the model.

The first step of the Structural Model is the process of identification of the incorrect pattern of behavior. In this process the therapist gathers the initial interview. In Structural Pattern Reframing model, the therapist looks for a specific information concerning the pattern of behavior. By asking questions therapist also puts the problem into specific framework and starts the initial work with the perspective in which a patient perceives their problems.

On the second stage, the preparation for the departure from the old pattern of behavior is being secured. The aim of this stage is to create within a patient a potential for future change. One is doing it by working with the way patient perceives the problem. The therapist works further with the perspective which the patient uses to talk about the problem. The goal is to diminish the impact and strength of the old interpretation and old pattern of behavior on the subject. The new frame of reference is being introduced and established for the problem behavior to enable new creative insights into the problem and to stimulate alternative understandings and ways of dealing with the problem to occur.

The third stage is the natural consequence of the successful completion of the second one. The patient starts to see the behavior as maladaptive and the therapist focuses their attempts on breaking the old pattern of behavior, together with the client. In this stage, the therapist underlines the positive aspects and needs standing behind the pattern of behavior, the ones that the pattern does not fulfill or fulfills in a way that causes a lot of discomfort to the patient or their environment. Then, the patient and the therapist, together in the process of exploration of the problem within the new framework, discover that the maladaptive pattern of behavior satisfies neither the needs nor goals of the patient and stays in contradiction to them. Then the pattern is being detached from the needs and the readiness for some new input is being secured. There is an empty gap that needs to be fulfilled with some new way of dealing with the given part of reality.

With the fourth stage, the therapist fills the gap with the new pattern of behavior, designed in such a way to fulfill the key needs and goals of the patient standing behind the old pattern of behavior. On this stage the therapist introduces the new pattern and incorporates the old needs in it. Then, they may compare it to the old pattern and show to the patient the differences. This will ensure the patient that the old pattern is maladaptive and reorient them more towards the new way of reacting. In the end of this step, the therapist secures the acceptance of the new pattern of behavior and new framework connected to it.

The fifth stage consists of activities that will project the pattern into the future, thus securing its good functioning through time.

The therapist designs here the multi-modal visualizations to project the pattern into the future. They also set some assignments and create activities so that the patient would be able to experience the pattern in action. All of these reinforce the still fragile and new structure created in the course of the structural treatment.

In such an approach we can see some similarities with previously described paradigms. The first and second step taken together reflect, in some way, the first stage of the model of intervention described by Milton H. Erickson (Erickson & Rossi, 1979) in which the therapist gathers the information about the problem and the frame of reference of the patient, as well as establishes the new frame of reference! The period of therapeutic trance is in some ways a reflection of the third and fourth stage of the Structural Model, where the therapist breaks the pattern of behavior and introduces new possibilities. And finally, the third stage of Erickson's model - the ratification of therapeutic trance reflects in some way the last step of the Structural Model, the reinforcement of the new pattern of behavior period.

The figure below presents the detailed comparison of the mentioned above models with the one presented within this book.

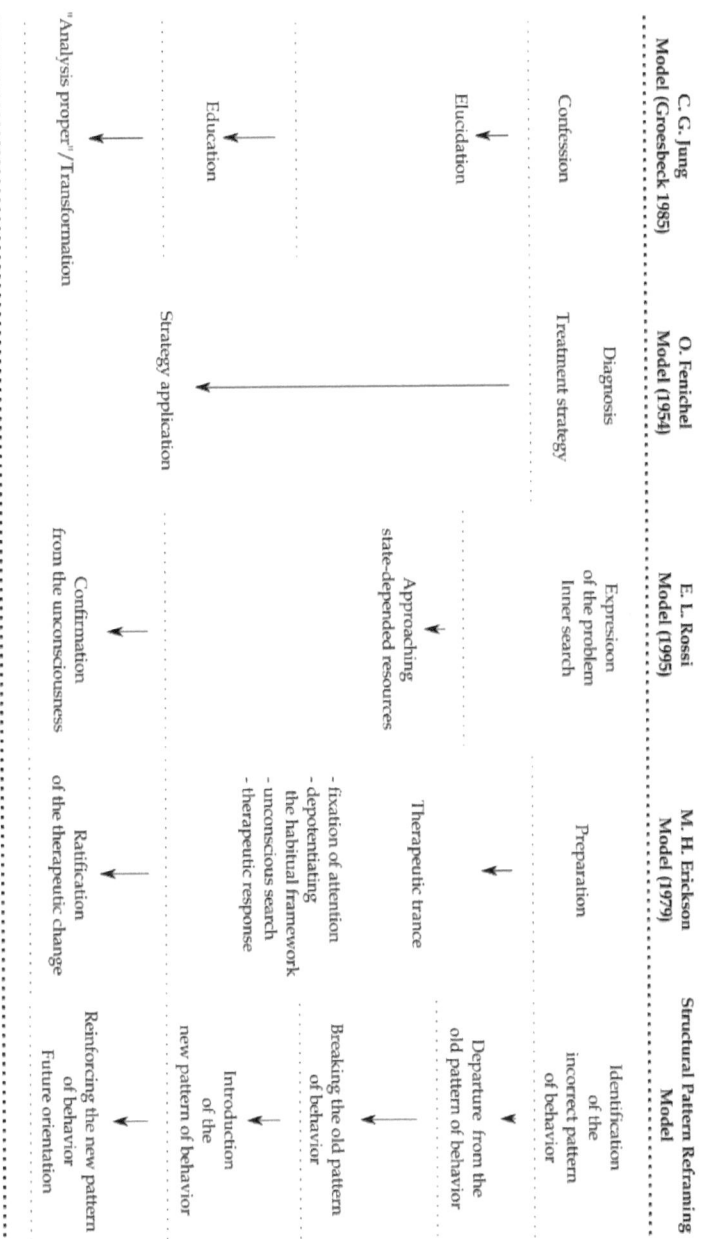

Figure 2: the comparison between all previously presented models. It demonstrates some similarities as well as differences among the models. Stages on the same level (height) are considered quite similar in nature.

4

THE STRUCTURAL PATTERN REFRAMING MODEL

1.The identification of an incorrect pattern of behavior

In each and every case of therapy, the therapeutic process has to start some place in order to carry on some dynamics and achieve some goals. Depending on the approach, the therapist uses in their work, the first session can take on a totally different course and end up in a totally different way. In case of the Structural Pattern Reframing model, the therapist will focus in the process of diagnosis on calling forth the structural determinants of the problem. They will try to put the problem in a framework of the pattern of behavior described in the first part. Let us now take a close look on the process together.

The first stage of the intervention begins at the moment when the patient enters the office of the therapist, or in the situation of a group therapy, when the person expresses the willingness to work on their problem in the group. The main task in this stage is to gather the information about the problem, and to start the reformulation of it. This reformulation should lead us to the point where the problem will be defined in some kind of solvable terms. And the last but very important thing that the therapist needs to achieve before entering the next step is the patient's acceptance for the new reality in which the old pattern is nested, or in other words, for the new interpretation of the problem behavior.

Gathering the information about the problem behavior

In most therapeutic situations, the first thing the therapist does is gathering the therapeutic interview. The patient comes into the office with some ideas and understandings of the problem. The interview, in general, has to give us a clear picture of what we are dealing with. Based in different psychotherapeutic paradigms, different psychotherapists would ask about different things and would require different information from the client to start working on the actual problem. The behaviorists would most certainly ask questions which would unveil for them the behaviors that needs to be changed, as well as the sources of rewards and punishments. In the field of psychoanalysis, therapists would ask a lot of questions uncovering the past experiences of the patient, especially from the early age. In Structural Pattern Reframing the questions asked in this phase has two separate functions. First one is to uncover the pattern of behavior that we are dealing with, and second is to reframe the problem so that it would be viewed by the patient as solvable.

Now, we will try to answer the question about what kind of questions we should ask the patient. As we remember from the chapter dedicated to the idea of the pattern of behavior, it has some core features. First of all, the pattern can manifest itself in a series of seemingly not connected in any way behaviors, but it always has a unique base, some underlying principle, that the therapist needs to uncover or build.

For example, when the wife is extremely jealous about the husband, she will display a lot of different behaviors. She may, for instance, shout at him when she will feel that she can get to him in any different way. She may also try to control him in a variety of ways or dominate him. The basis of all these behaviors could be some frustrated needs, like need for love or feeling significant to him. The answer to a question why these needs are so important to the subject and why he or she reacts in such a way when these are frustrated may lay deep in the history of the patient or somewhere in the current relationship. And so, the pattern underlying all this behaviors and giving them conjoined ground is based on satisfying the need for love or the feeling of being important for the partner. The definition of behaviors presented by the wife in terms of frustration of the need for love reframes the whole problem to the patients and gives them at the start point some new possibilities. That process occurs due to the fact that all behaviors start with a frustration of some need and are a response, a way to bring back the equilibrium. At many occasions the client feels the discomfort about a way they deal with a problem, but do not see it in a broader context. That blocks the change from happening. The patient is stuck in their pattern of behavior. The introduction of the needs enables a person to redesign the behavior. The patient may, together with the therapist, figure out better, more adaptive ways of satisfying that need.

Secondly, the pattern leads us to some outcome. The need is being satisfied by it. One person does something to another. In this case, for example, husband stays home and the wife feels safe and taken care of. On some occasions, for instance, the depression serves some patients to put some pressure on another person or people. The depression pattern brings a lot of benefits to the patient, like, for example, care, attention of others, one can also punish someone by behaving in a depressive manner, there are a lot of possibilities within the patterns of depression.

In general, the pattern always leads to a satisfaction of some need or needs, which means that the person displaying it has always some benefits from it, even if it is generally painful for that person.

The therapist needs to determine the following things with the questions they will ask the client:

> How does the pattern look like? What kind of behaviors are involved in it?
>
> Why does a patient do what s/he does?
>
> What is the underlying core need or reason which sets the pattern up and brings it to life?

Secondary, the therapist needs to determine the benefits, which patient pulls out from the pattern.

> What kind of needs are being satisfied, what kind of goals are being achieved?
>
> In what way are the needs being satisfied?

The therapist needs to remember these few simple objectives while asking questions. When asking about the pattern and its properties and parameters, one can avoid many additional questions that could direct the work on different track. For example, in the case of depression some therapists tend to ask many content driven questions.

The patient enters the office and in the initial interview declares:

"I have a depression"

and the therapist responses:

"About what?"

This is an example of the content question. Typical response will be: About many things. Or about this and that... And at that point we enter into the content analysis. It may be of some use to understand the patient fully or to specify some parts of the reality to make them less general and more specific. It does not give us, however, any information about the pattern standing behind it. Content has a secondary meaning in the Structural Pattern Reframing. Pattern operates according to simple rules, and it always uses some content. But through changing the content we will not change the patterns. The result will most likely be that we will be discarding the content and the pattern will utilize another content unit or will have tendency to go back to the old understandings. That is why we should avoid content based questions, and focus on the structure instead. One is not supposed, however, to mix it up with the techniques proposed by Cognitive Behavioral Approach (Beck et al., 1985, 1979), which indeed focus on discarding the thoughts and unveiling incoherence in the process of thinking, this is, however, also in a way structural work, because its goal is to discard the maladaptive thinking pattern. Therapists in this situation may use these kind of techniques to block the pattern and break it by showing its inconsistency with, for example, external facts. Notice, however, that this kind of work does not focus on the content but rather uses it to illustrate the way a pattern works.

The constructive role of language and reality relativity

The way in which a therapist formulates and communicates

their ideas is also a matter of great importance. The therapist may notice and capture a lot of important information about the way a patient perceives his/her problem from the way s/he formulates their statements. In general, a therapist and a patient influence one another with the way they communicate.

Now, that we know what kind of information is important for us to diagnose and change the pattern of behavior, we can discus another property of the questions. On one side, the questions are giving the therapist information necessary to work with the pattern but, on the other hand, the same questions shape in a way the context of the problem for the patient. Whorf (1956) was one of the first researchers focusing on the creational role of language in our reality. In his relativity hypothesis he pointed out that the language we use and live in shapes our experience and perception of the surrounding world. The amount of categories and dimensions we are familiar with, and use to describe our experience, determines what we see, feel and remember. In other words, Eskimos for instance, know more than twenty different kinds of snow and are able to distinguish between them, when, at the same time, people from the western cultures do not possess such knowledge. There are people in the world that cannot distinguish between blue and green, not because of some visual dysfunction, but because they do not have that kind of distinction in their language. O'Hanlon (1990) points out that the therapist educated in a specific current of psychotherapy like, for example, psychoanalysis, gestalt or whichever, will use a language of this school to describe the problems of their patients. Pretty soon the patients will start to have gestalt- psychoanalytical- or, for example, cognitive-behavioral- kinds of problems.

In Structural Pattern Reframing we adapt this constructivist point of view on the language. There are two assumptions from it. First of all, the structure of language itself will give us a lot of additional information about how the patient sees his problem, and secondly, the process of asking questions is not a passive extraction of information from the patient, but rather an active process of the reality creation.

Below, the author will present some parts of the structural model of pattern reframing concerning this first stage and the art of formulating questions.

Asking questions – the art of reality shaping

To start the presentation of the art of asking questions, we have to adopt some basic assumptions, helpful in understanding the model.

First of all, the reality is being created all the time, and is being constantly defined and discovered by the process of interpretation and reinterpretation. Evidence for this assumption can be found in the following writings (Bandler & Grinder, 1975; Goffman, 2006; Watzlawick, 1978, 1990).

If so, the language has an active role in the process of reality creation (Bandler & Grinder, 1975, 1982; Watzlawick, Weakland, & Fish, 1974; Watzlawick, 1978, 1990; Whorf, 1956). It can change the perception of an event, reinforce or diminish the current vision of the reality.

Now, we can pass on to the main part of our language patterns. The material presented below was most likely in parts replicated in some other studies, but some parts of it, are also in a way new. The author will now describe few patterns one by one, so that a reader would be able to master them one by one. In the reality, where we approach a client, we cannot make such an artificial distinctions. All this patterns are supposed to be used in a conjoined fashion and be specially tailored to the patient and their own realities and situation they are in. Another thing one should remember is that these patterns are useful and helpful on every stage of the intervention. The author decided to discuss it in details in this section due to the main role of asking good questions in this entry level of the session, where the reality of the problem is being defined.

Working with perspective

The perspective is a feature of a language, which is directly connected to the way one perceives the problem situation. People will most certainly enter the office with some hypothesis on what is going on to them. These hypothesis include certain view on the problem which manifests in the language patterns. It may be in part conscious, but the language patterns are mostly unconsciously driven. People will describe their problems as more or less global, overwhelming, difficult, hard to overcome and so on. All this ideations will be reflected in the way a patient talks about the problem, in categories s/he uses to talk about it. These are all the features of the inner world of the patient, and the problem which is always nested somewhere within this world. Moreover, sometimes the patient will describe their problem in a seemingly neutral way, without emotions, without stress, but still the therapist will somehow fill the weight of a problem. The reason for it is that the patient, even though he or she does not manifest the emotions outside, will use special kind of language patterns in their description and the therapist will unconsciously perceive the description as emotionally overwhelming or very difficult and hard to overcome. Usually, a person who listens to another people's confession about the problem is focused on the content; he or she wants to extract as much as possible from the story to provide to another the feeling of being listened to and to create the impression of being a good, supporting and alert listener, as well as to enable an effect of catharsis to the patient. At the same time, it is the structure which affects the person unconsciously. Some language features, like for example nominalizations (Bandler & Grinder, 1975), or global statements (Weiner, 1992) will create the impression on a listener, where the problem will be perceived as difficult and hard due to the globalization processes, and unsolvable due to the processes of nominalization, which takes away the dynamics of a process, and creates from it an object. More on the process of nominalization, the reader can read in the part of this chapter dedicated specially to this subject.

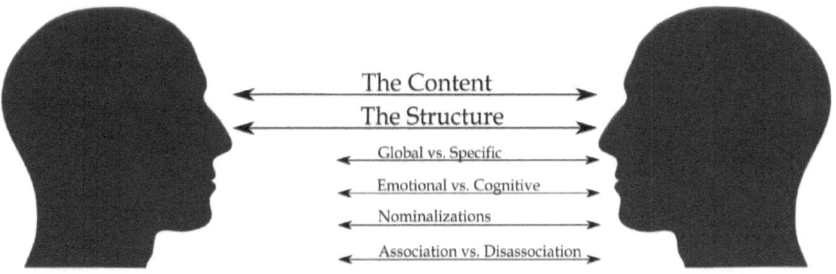

Figure 3: The multiple levels of communication. Within any communication process one can distinguish at least two levels of communication. The content of the communication reflects what one person wants to communicate to another. The structure of the communication reflects how that person formulates the information. It also reflects the way a person constructs and perceives the reality around themselves.

All the features of patients' particular way of expression may be used to extract more details about the structure of their inner perception of the problem. This information may also be used to change the meaning and the weight of the problem. On this step of the intervention, the therapist may use a lot of different tools like paraphrasing or summarizing what patient says to input slight changes of meaning. One achieves this goal by applying the principles of the perspective shifting described below.

In the following publication, two main complementary ways of working with the perspective were identified. One was called, the Spiral Model of Perspective Shifting, and the second the Dimensional Model of Perspective Shifting. Below the reader will find a short but complete description of these two ways of working. The author strongly advises not to treat them, however, as some separate paradigms, as they were divided to provide clear description, and make the process of learning and understanding more clear. In practice, however, these two work together and in various configurations.

Spiral Model of Perspective Shifting

One way of perspective shifting is described as a spiral model. The model seizes the perspective in the form of a spiral. The more we move towards the centre of the spiral, the more specific the perspective becomes. The more we go away from the centre, the more the perspective becomes general, including more elements into the set. To enter a higher level on the spiral, the therapist introduces more general quantifiers into the description the patient gives about the problem. To enter a lower level, therapist introduces more specific quantifiers. The therapist may achieve this by asking questions or using a paraphrasing technique, for example.

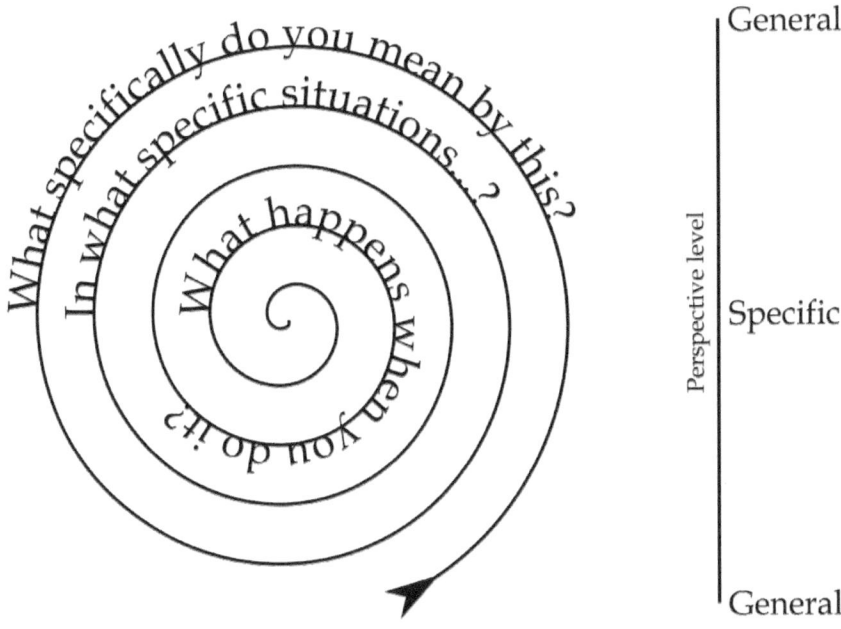

Figure 4: The general schema of the spiral model of perspective shifting. Consecutive questions bring the problem from more general level (outer part of the spiral) to more specific (the center of the spiral), making it at the same time more detailed and limited to specific circumstances.

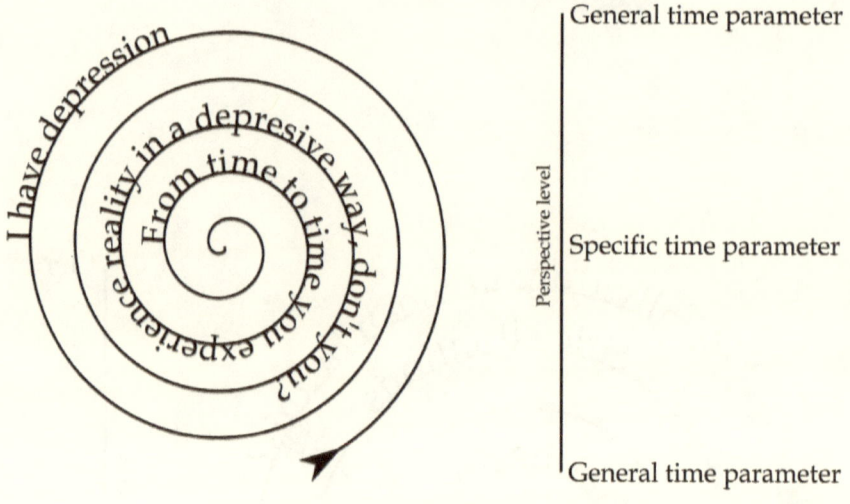

Figure 5: The general schema of the spiral model of perspective shifting utilizing paraphrase as a tool to change time parameter. By adding the time parameter "from time to time" to the patients description, the procedure makes it less general. The unspecified time parameter in the statement "I have depression" was substituted with "from time to time" parameter. Additionally, the referential point was brought back to the patient (from outer reality) with the reframing from "I have" to "you experience".

Many times people enter into the therapeutic situation with very general statements related to their problems. For example, they can start with such statements as:

"I have phobia" or "I'm afraid of people" or "I have depression"

These are very general statements, which affect large variety of elements and classes within very general sets. Approaching the center of the spiral, or making the problem more specific can be achieved by specifying questions like these, for example:

1. What specifically do You mean by this? – it is a general question forcing more specific inner search into a problem structure.

2. In what specific situations are you afraid of people? – the question precise more specific situations in which the symptom occurs.

3. What happens when You do this? – this question specify what exactly happens during the time a client calls phobia, depression etc. It also brings back the referential point into the subject. The patient does something rather than something happens to the patient. The implication of this is that one can do something with it. It is much more difficult to get under control something which happens to us, outside of us, than something which is inside, a part of our behavior or expression. More on this subject can be read in the part about the nominalization process.

Generally speaking, the questions specifying the problem situation shift the perspective down, making it more specific.

Another way to shift the perspective down is to paraphrase the statement in such a way that it introduces some kind of calibration or specification. In the example presented above where the patient declares:

I have depression

The therapist may, for example, paraphrase that statement in such a way:

From time to time You experience reality in a depressive way, don't you?

This is a redirecting paraphrase, which, if accepted, changes the perception of the problem in two ways. It introduces the concept of "from time to time", which indirectly introduces possibilities of other ways of perceiving the reality. It also changes the depression nominalization into the process of "experiencing reality in a depressive manner". For further discussion on the nominalization process see the part of this chapter dedicated to the dimensional perspective shifting.

Sometimes, however, we want to expand the perspective in some direction, for example, to expand the point of view of some sort, and include into it some new possibilities. We can simply ask questions about additional elements of the possible set to do this. For example:

Patient: I feel terrified about tomorrow tests.

Therapist: What other emotions do You feel?

That kind of question will possibly provoke an inner search. We cannot, however, predict the direction towards which it will lead us. The depressive patient will, for example, show a tendency to overrate the value of negative associations, and because of the following, will create more and more negative connotations. On the other hand, when we specify another parameter of this question and ask, for example:

"What kind of other positive emotions could one feel in such a situation?"

we will most likely meet with the resistance of some kinds, or simply will hear "none" as an answer. The author proposes another way of perspective shifting towards some expansion. One can use a simple paraphrase and add to it some desired qualities. For example, if one would like to expand a perspective of a patient suffering from a depression, or rather, presenting a set of depressive patterns of behavior, one can put it as follow:

"When you do it, you feel sad and depressed, and You also feel a lot of other sensations."

The first part of this sentence is a change of the nominalization into process, further we do have pacing statements (feel sad and depressed). These help the therapist maintain a rapport and create feeling of understanding. It is important to use the patient's words as a pacing statements. We do not want to expand their negative associations in this case. The last part of the sentence serves as the expansion of the set of categories. It introduces the concept of some other emotions. One can further direct the attention of a client towards desired understandings by further implications.

"Some of these emotions are strong, some are very mild, some can be very neutral, almost unnoticeable, some others may be a bit more positive..."

By adding these possibilities we also utilize the phenomenon of priming or otherwise called seeding (Zeig, 1990). According to the research on priming and seeding, the exposition of the stimuli itself influences the patient by increasing the availability of the concept inside of the patients mind. So, only by mentioning certain possibilities, we invite them into the patient inner world and expand their range of possible choices.

Dimensional Model of Perspective shifting

Another way of perspective shifting may be achieved by applying the dimensional model's principles. The basic idea standing behind this model is that people operate on various dimensions while describing and perceiving the reality. On some occasions, the description of a problem shows a tendency to polarize on one of two ends of the dimension. For example, a person may describe the problem in a global way, creating the impression that the problem is huge and affects all walks of life, or they can use very specific examples, thus being unable to see that something happened more than once. If the therapist notices such a tendency of polarization they may, using the dimensional model, shift the perspective more towards a state of equilibrium.

A person entering the office will most certainly start describing the problem using certain attributes. These attributes may be grouped into few dimensions. The therapist may easily identify these dimensions and develop or change them by asking adequately constructed questions.

The author will now shortly describe few of these dimensions and suggest possible directions in working with them. This classification, however, neither drains the topic nor it pretends to be perceived as complete. The subject is just presented here for the first time, as a result of a research project, and needs further research to be developed and verified.

Nominalization – process

The phenomenon of nominalization in language was firstly introduced to the field of psychotherapy by Richard Bandler and John Grinder(1975) in a first volume of the book called "The Structure of Magic". They describe the nominalization as one of the processes of distortion within the language. The nominalization mainly disconnects some experience from the ongoing process, making it stiff. The nominalization is perceived by the subject as exterior and at many times overwhelming. The possibility to maintain or change the process in some desired direction is perceived as being outside of the patients range of influence or control. Nominalization is generally a noun describing an event or a process. Words like: depression, phobia, schizophrenia, marriage, sadness, are all the direct examples of nominalizations. Patients will also use phrases like:

{some nominalization} happens to me on many occasions

{some nominalization} occurs...

These and similar expressions represent the nominalization phenomenon. The author prefers slightly different view on this subject than presented by Bandler and Grinder (1975), where the nominalization was described as a transformation of process into a noun. In this book, the nominalization is defined as an inner process of pulling the responsibility for an action outside from the subject. In the process of nominalization our own inner processes, actions become exterior to us, and we lose control over them. We do not do, make or create - we have. This is the major difference. If the patient declares:

"I have a depression"

Their ability of controlling these patterns of behavior is minimal or none. They indeed have something and do not do anything. In such a case, how can they do anything about this?

The nominalization usually creates an impression about the event of being general and outside of patients influence range. In some cases, the therapist may like to create some nominalizations, but mostly we would like to dismantle the nominalization, and bring back the flow of the process within the patient. By bringing the process back to the client, we restore within them the feeling of control over the event, as well as we put the referential point back to the patient. The depression, or phobia or anything else no longer happens to the patient. The patient does something. The question then becomes why are they doing it? What kind of benefits can they bring from it? What other ways of satisfying the goal or need can they undertake to accomplish it in more satisfactory way? These are totally different questions coming from the mindset with the processes brought back to its place (into the subject). These questions are only possible to be asked and worked on, on further steps of the Structural Pattern Reframing Model, after changing the nominalization into process, as well as maintaining other things described further in this book.

To change the nominalizations into processes, the therapist must at first mark them down and then use specially designed questions to bring back the process. Nominalizations are generally manifested in the language of the patient in the form of nouns (Bandler & Grinder, 1975). Words like depression, phobia, fear, generally all the DSM or ICD diagnostic manual categories, are nominalizations. The nominalization is something you cannot see in the real world, cannot touch it or talk to it. One cannot see love, for example. One can infer about it from a specific set of behaviors. Things like depression, phobia or any other clinical category, are just sets of specific behaviors or patterns of behavior. So, a nominalization can be recognized by the fact, that it is being referred to as physical object, when it is not really a one of such kind. Bandler and Grinder (1975) proposed a very simple way of distinguishing between real nouns and nominalizations.

"True nouns will not fit into the blank in the phrase {an ongoing _____}, in a well formed way."

(Bandler & Grinder, 1975 p. 72)

For example, an ongoing depression or phobia fits well, and an ongoing table or glass does not, due to the fact that it is a real noun.

Now, that we know how to notice the nominalizations, we need to know the way of changing them back into processes. The author proposes to do it in an indirect way, without marking the clear distinction of the procedure. To do it, one has to ask special kind of questions. The questions which are to be answered require from the patient to bring back the referential point inside, from the outside.

When a patient says: "I have phobia," the referential point is outside of them somewhere. They refer to something as being outside of them, in this case a phobia. To do it, one has to create the nominalization, an object, in which one could place the referential point to which one could refer. The question that would bring the referential point back to the patient and would abolish the nominalization has to refer to an action. The example:

Patient: I have phobia

Therapist: what happens in a specific situation *when You do it?*

If the patient would like to answer this question, they have to think of their phobia in terms of a process. They need to think about the problem in terms of what happens when they do the phobia set. What do I do specifically? How do I react on my own actions or patterns?

When the patient responds to the question, they accepts unconsciously the assumption that something is happening within them; that it is something they do, more than something that happens to them. Of course, many times one can answer to the therapist with some further nominalizations. Then the procedure is the same, we ask about it in terms of a process. For example:

Patient: I have phobia

Therapist: what happens in a specific situation *when You do it?*

Patient: I have dizziness and trembling.

Therapist: how long do You need to tremble and feel dizzy?

Patient: How long? I don't know. Quite a while.

The change that occurs within the patient after asking that question is more complex than only the nominalization shift. We bring the referential point back to the patient. S/he trembles and feels dizzy. These are the processes within the patient and, therefore, are more easy to be controlled, even if the patient still does not know it consciously. Another shift occurring in the second question is the implication that the patient needs it for some reason. Consciously this part was probably ignored or unnoticed by the patient at this time, but unconsciously probably it was noticed, or even accepted, due to the fact, that we do not see any manifestation of the resistance.

Association – dissociation

The term dissociation is used on the field of psychology and psychiatry in many different ways. Most common use is presented within the context of the conversion disorders presented as in DSM-IV-TR (American Psychiatric Association, 1994). But we will not be using here this term in its pathological meaning.

Another way of speaking about the dissociation was developed in the field of the Neurolinguistic Programming (Andreas & Andreas, 1989; Bandler, 1992). In this model the dissociation and association are connected to the way one can experience the imaginary situation. Within the NLP theoretical framework, one distinguishes between the representation systems and submodalities (Bandler & MacDonald, 1988; Grinder, DeLozier, & Bandler, 1977). Representational systems are the modalities through which one can experience the outside world. One can, for example, perceive the world through the visual submodality and in consequence create the visual representation of the experience in their mind. The same can be done on auditory, kinesthetic and olfactory dimensions. In NLP generally speaking, it is postulated, that there is a possibility of determining the dominant representation system (Grinder et al., 1977), a person, or a client uses most commonly to perceive the reality. Many times to avoid the resistance or gain a rapport with the unconscious mind, the therapist will use the least used representational system to formulate suggestions in therapy. The dissociation can be explained in this context, for example, in terms of the visual representational system as a way of gaining a distance from something. In the fast phobia cure technique (Andreas & Andreas, 1989; Bandler, 1992) for example, a patient is asked to do the dissociation by stepping out of the image he sees, and see it, for example, like in the cinema. In some other forms (Bandler, 1992) the patient can be asked just to see himself from the outside, like in the movie. The association is gained by reversing the process and asking a patient to step "into his own shoes" and see the situation with his own eyes. One can notice that this operations are mainly performed in the described form on the Visual representation system. Similar can be done on other modalities.

In more Ericksonian approach, Michael Yapko (2002) describes the dissociation as an ability to separate some elements one from another. In this viewpoint the patients with depression, for example, many times have problems with proper application of this mechanism in their life. The example of this can be found, when such a person will perceive, for instance, the whole day or event of a kind in a dark pessimistic fashion, simply because one bad thing occurred. The same event, on the other hand, provided a person with a lot of possibilities for joy and happiness, but the inability to dissociate the one negative experience enables it to dominate the perception in a way so that the depressive person will not notice any positive things in the situation. At the same time the patient disassociated the positive experiences from the general situation.

In Structural Pattern Reframing Model the dimension Association – Dissociation in generally defined as being more attached or detached from some experience. One can lead a person from an associated state to dissociated, causing the event, or in other words, an element of the structure to bring not so vivid and strong emotions. On some other occasions a therapist would like to associate more a client with some memories, creating stronger bound with these and enabling them to influence a patient more. The association with the long forgotten possibilities can be observed during many sessions of Dr. Milton H. Erickson when he was evoking the early learning set (Erickson et al., 1976). Many times also, on another occasions, Erickson would regress the patient back to the childhood and put them through some experiences to bring back some long forgotten resources, useful for future changes (detailed examples with commentary can be found in Zeig, 1980b). In such a way the therapist may put a person through some experience, bringing back all the emotions, sensations and many more. In this way the patient re-associates with the experience. Mainly to re-associate the patient with some disassociated part, a therapist needs to put them in some way through that experience, using hypnotic regression, visualization or, for instance, some assignments that will include some activity through which a patient may re-experience some emotions and feelings.

Cognition – Emotion

The dimension between cognition and emotion is another way of perceiving reality and perspective shifting. It can change the perception from more distant analytic one to more emotionally driven, and back. This distinction is based on the neurological difference between right and left hemisphere in the brain. Due to some authors (Rossi, 1995) the brain neurological structure can be clearly divided into two separate parts, among the hemispheric division. The right hemisphere is associated with more emotional as well as creative ways of thinking, and left hemisphere is more involved into logical rational ways of analyzing information. On the basis of this distinction, some authors postulate, that there are different ways of communication depending on how we want to affect the brain (Watzlawick, 1978). These ways can also be noted in language as different ways of communication. The left hemisphere language is the language of reason and logic. The right hemisphere patterns of communication are more emotionally driven. The metaphor is one of the examples of the right hemisphere ways of communication (S. R. Lankton & Lankton, 1983; Mills & Crowley, 1986). In Structural Pattern Reframing, this dimension is reflected in two positions, perceptual and emotional, or as Anthony Robbins(Robbins & Madanes, 2005a, 2005b) refers to it - the perspective of a heart and a mind. This distinction does not necessarily reflects the amount of emotions expressed during the act of communication. The amount of emotions is more likely connected with the association – dissociation dimension, described above. The heart - mind dimension is more likely associated with the way one perceives the reality he or she describes in the moment. When one describes the reality from the standpoint of the mind, they analyze the event, including the past events. Therefore, the mind perspective is more judgmental. When one refers to the past, he is looking into many similarities in their perception events, and puts them all into one cognitive category. The moment a person puts a label on that kind of set of events, the judgment is created. In this perspective, the person is evaluating current situation from a perspective of set of events. Judgmental viewpoint is sometimes useful, especially when one evaluates their own behaviors. Sometimes, however, it blocks our perception and puts it into a frame of a kind, which tends to disable alternative explanations. The negative consequences of "being in head" are: the judgmental and sometimes conflicting standpoint, stress and incoherence. The perspective shifting from mind or head to heart invites totally different perspective(Robbins & Madanes, 2005b), as well as creates a physiological coherence changing the point of view biologically (McCraty, Atkinson, & Tomasino, 2001; McCraty, Atkinson, Tomasino, & Bradley, 2006). Changing the perspective from cognitively driven to the one which "comes from the heart" disables the judgmental mental set (Robbins & Madanes, 2005b), and creates an emotionally driven perspective focused on now, and on the feelings coming from the heart and not on judgments and analysis from the brain. The experience of the author supports this statements. This is a very powerful shift, which brings a lot of new and more constructive understandings for the present situation.

To work on this dimension, the therapist should first notice it within a clients communication repertoire. To do it, one should focus on the way in which a patient formulates his statements. Many times the client will use phrases like: I think..., in my opinion..., and so forth. This kind of statements usually forego judgmental statements. Another useful direction is to mark down if the patient refers to the past in his statements. Almost all the time when patient creates an evaluation of the situation they refer to some past events. The reference happens when we hear something more than what we see. The example can represent the following statement of a client's:

"He is not listening to me now!"

This statement was an answer of a woman on a specific face expression of her husband's. Of course, when she made that statement, she referred to the past experiences. The expression itself does not give us enough information to create such a judgment, without past context attached to it.

The question that can be useful to tell the difference between past-derived and non-past-derived statement is:

Am I able to create a statement based on the information I perceive at the moment?

If the answer is no, we do have a reference to the past.

Another manifestation of being "in the brain" is when someone uses expressions like: "I will now tell you how it is for real'. That kind of statement usually indicated some point of view on a problem, most likely it also introduces some judgments, especially when the problem is shared among more than one person.

It is very important to detect and mark down the currently used pole of the dimension. The first step on the way to change it from cognitive to emotional is to notice it and introduce the distinction into the patient's inner world. One can do it by simply pointing it out. This will give them the possibility of choice between the two ways of perception. It does not mean they will shift the perspective right away, but at least they will be aware of such an option.

The most effective way of introducing the emotional perspective is to create an experience that will demonstrate to the client an alternative way of thinking. In the core of the emotional perspective, there is an emotion, so there is no better way of demonstrating than by experiencing it.

In the following example, one can observe the procedure of introducing the emotional perspective into the discourse of the patient.

> Patient: he does not listen to me at all. Any conversation is pointless, he always knows best.

Now, in this statement we clearly see a lot of generalizations and references to the past events. He does not behave in such a way now, but previously there were events from which the patient came with such a conclusion and impression. One can do a lot of things to change such a perception.

> Therapist: do You mean that he does not hear what You are saying at a precise moment in time?

At that moment the therapist explores deeper the concept of listening. The information about what the patient understands by it can bring a valuable insight into the situation.

> Patient: No! he just stands there, and does nothing, and then goes away. I feel like I've been alone in there.

> Therapist: You feel like alone when he is standing there so closed inside of him, don't you?

> Patient: Yes.

At this point a patient accepts, though probably not consciously new elements introduced into his inner world. Now, we are working here with the feeling of being alone, and with the isolation of the partner.

> Therapist: why do you think he closes himself in such a way?

Patient: I do not know? Because he does not care?

Therapist: What You just did is a judgmental statement. You do it when You are in your head, instead of in Your heart. Do you know the difference?

Here the therapist introduces the distinction between the emotional and cognitive perspective, in a metaphor of mind and heart. This metaphor was also used by Anthony Robbins in his interventions, to seed this distinction(Robbins & Madanes, 2005b).

Patient: not really.

Therapist: You observe the reality, you analyze it, and you create a vision of this reality, you are in your head. You do quite a lot of work in there all the time. You connect experiences and ideas from Your past, and you create interpretation of the reality. It can be more or less accurate at times, but it serves a lot of purposes. Then, on the other hand, You can be in Your heart. When You are in your heart, you do not judge, you are with your emotions, now! In the presence of a specific moment. Do you know that state?

In this part of the talk, the therapist does a lot of things. He introduces at first the idea of cognitive frame. Then, he puts it in a context of being in the past. And then, he creates a space for some doubt and a place for something else by introducing the concept of accuracy. *It can be more or less accurate at times.* This is a statement that is difficult to reject. In the original Milton Erickson's work he calls it a truism (Erickson & Rossi, 1979), an obvious statement, that cannot be rejected. Everybody makes mistakes in their judgments from time to time. This introduces a possibility of making a mistake, and thus diminishes the strength of this dimension and of statements coming out of it.

Patient: Well, I'm in my head almost all the time.

Now, what we can see, is that the patient accepts new components of the inner reality by referring to them in their talk.

Therapist: Exactly. And when You are in your head, You can't be in Your heart at the same time. Now, to go there first, you have to feel the heart you have. Feel its beating. How well it works. The calm beats. You may even be willing to touch it. Feel its warmth spreading around.

Now the therapist builds the state based on feelings and sensations from the body, to focus the patient on emotions and its experience.

Therapist: you may even close your eyes, to go deeper and feel it all more and more inside.

It may take some time to build such a state within a subject. The patient then comes to the point in which they use the emotions to perceive and understand the situation. Let us now go further into the session and see how this all procedure shifted the perception of the patient.

Therapist: Now, feel the situation in which you talk with your partner. How is it?

Patient: (with tears in her eyes): it is sad, so sad.

Therapist: How does your partner feel? Go from your heart. What can he possibly feel?

Patient: Lonely... Misunderstood...

Therapist: and how do You feel?

Patient: the same...

Now, the therapist came into the new definition of the situation. The patient and her partner misinterpret their behaviors. This is totally different problem to deal with, then on the beginning, because it involves both people and requires work on both sides.

This case study, however, presents the idea about how to introduce the dimension cognition – emotion into the session and work with it. First, one should define the situation in the terms of the dimension, then one provides the difference between the poles of the dimension. Then, the experience of the neglected part of the dimension is introduced, which in consequence, shifts the meaning of the situation. One redefines the problem with the patient.

Global – local

The Global-Local dimension was at first proposed by Weiner (1992), in his theory of human motivation. According to it, people explain situations in a variety of ways, attaching the responsibility for occurrence of some events either to themselves or to some external factors. So, according to this theory, people can explain an event from the perspective of interior or exterior control point of view. In other words, one can perceive an event as something that they have done, or something that has happened to them. In Weiner's theory, this dimension is called the locus of control. Another dimension is controllability. It answers the question, whether an event is controllable. Sometimes people would perceive an event as easy to maintain and manage, and sometimes when it is viewed as out of their control, as not so easy. The third dimension can be called a stability through time. Is the event just an event or is it a tendency? - that is the question it answers. The Weiner's model (1992) answers the question of how people explain the reality around them. The origins of the dimension Global – Local can be found exactly in this theory. The global part of the dimension occurs when a patient explains and perceives an event as general problem, something that happens over and over again. Local events are these which happened one time, or something a patient has done once, at the precise point in time. Martin Seligman described a typical depressive pessimistic, and optimistic profile based on the Weiner's theory (Seligman, 2010). According to Seligman, pessimists would perceive bad events as long-lasting and affecting all walks of their lives. The responsibility for the presence of such an event they impose on themselves, of course. On the other hand, optimists would perceive the same events as limited in time to the specific event. The fault for its occurrence they would prescribe to some external factors or other people, but not to themselves. Many times they treat difficulties as challenges. One of the most important differences between these two ways of thinking is the one between local and global viewpoint on the events. One can change this dimension within a patient by paraphrasing his statement in more local or global fashion, depending on the intention. More global events would affect a person more, and more local will be perceived as easily managed. Usually we want to globalize the resourceful states and localize things which work in a destructive way for a patient.

To localize the statement we could also ask questions about a specific parameters of time and place in which an event took place, or we could ask about a frequency of the event and a time it usually lasts.

For instance when the patient indicates:

Patient: I experience constant attacks of aggression

The therapist may first of all observe the global general

perception by the use of word constant, and by absence of time parameters. Another important thing is a nominalization that probably disables a patient to take more control over the behavior. The therapist may at first specialize the time parameter by asking:

> Therapist: Where and when exactly do You experience your attacks?

The therapist may specify the length of an attack as well by asking:

> Therapist: How long does it take for You to start behaving in this way, and when does it usually start and stop?

Notice that in this particular question above the therapist specified a lot of the pattern parameters like time of duration of the behavior, its beginning and ending points, as well as he deconstructed the nominalization thus changing it back into process.

By asking such specifying questions we consequently lead our patient to a more local and less general way of thinking. This particular dimension has a lot in common with the previously discussed model of spiral perspective shifting, and therefore, one may supplement the other. The difference between these two is, that they are two constructs from separate orders. The general model of spiral perspective shifting is a way of meaning change, or of the reframing that can be used on virtually any content to change its perception. The dimension global - local serves us to observe specific tendency of the subject to frame some event or class of events in a particular, more globally or locally oriented way. After noticing the patient's tendency, it gives us the idea of towards which pole we would like to direct patient more for their own benefits.

Feminine – masculine

Feminine – Masculine is a dimension primarily observed within the work of Anthony Robbins (Robbins & Madanes, 2004b). The two edges of this dimension can be defined as follows: Femininity is connected to vulnerability and fragility. The masculinity is more connected with decisiveness and some other man's qualities. The most important thing, however, here is not what the content of the masculine or feminine categories is, but rather where one is placed on the dimension. Generally according to Sandra Bem (2000), the author of Gender Schema Theory, the people who are androgynic (posses well developed both feminine and masculine side) in nature are best adjusted. They can fit well into a variety of different situations and have much wider and more flexible repertoire of reactions and behaviors. The tendency of a particular person to associate more with a particular side of the dimension one can judge from the way they are dressed, more masculine or feminine; from the way they interact, from gestures, mimics, body posture. All of these can be more masculine or feminine in nature. The author will not provide a reader here with some simple directions on how to estimate someone's place on this dimension. Sometimes we can just see somehow that someone is too masculine or too feminine. The reason for it is, from the experience of the author, because the patient suppressed the other side due to some past events, and/or he or she does not notice the value of the side of this dimension that is suppressed. Many times presented high level of masculinity is, in fact, a way to cover up some weakness or pain that happened to be present in the past. It is important to notice such a thing, and to provide a person with some experiences which would enable them to feel the other side and unblock it. It is also very important to notate the reason why there is a tendency towards one side of the dimension and to reframe it in such a way to provide new understandings for the situation and secure the readiness for a change within a person. The therapist is supposed to reframe the situation in such a way so that the patient would be able to see what he or she misses by only using one side of this dimension and so that the patient would be able to see the benefits of using both sides.

One can also enable a person to become more balanced on this dimension by using hypnotic regression or techniques of visualization in purpose of associating the person with the neglected part. Another good idea is to provide a person with experiences or home assignments that will require a that person to use the neglected part of the dimension to complete the task.

Main targets of the first stage of the intervention

At this point we need to address the topic of what we need to accomplish in the first stage of the structural intervention to be able to move further. The main goal of the first step of the intervention is to create a reality for a change. It means we need to put a patient's problem into some context where we will proceed with further work. Paul Watzlawick (1990) claims that there is no problem before the definition of it. The patient usually comes to the therapist office with a mild idea that something is wrong. It is, therefore, our responsibility as therapists to define the reality of the problem to the patient in a change promoting way.

Now, what does it mean to create a change promoting problem reality? The first thing that one could have in mind is that it should be time limited. That, since we want it to be fast, we should place a time limit on it somehow. It is true that sometimes it helps. One of the leading authors in the field of Neuro-Linguistic Programming, Tad James (James, Flores, & Schober, 2006) writes that one should limit the length of the therapy by putting events in a time frame. For example, we can say that the problem we need to deal with will take three sessions to be resolved. Such a statement will provide a patient with a guideline for a change. He or she can now proceed somehow through the course of three sessions. There are two risks in such an approach however, that a therapist should take into consideration. First of all, the patient may not fully adjust to the time frame and go beyond, making the treatment ineffective in a given time perspective. It may result in a situation, where the therapist may lose some of the respect, the aura of competence, in the eyes of the patient. If the patient reacts to suggestion in a resistant manner, opposite to the content of suggestion s/he may purposely or unconsciously postpone the change process to prove something to themselves or to the therapist. Another problem that the author addresses here only briefly is the readiness for a change within a patient. We need to remember that, no matter what pattern we are dealing with, it is always in some way fulfilling some need or a goal. This means it has a function in a general system of the patient. If we would like to change it too quickly, we may evoke a resistance within a patient. This can stop the therapeutic process completely at the moment. So, no matter what we do, one should always remember to respect the inner reality of the patient's problem and all its ingredients. Otherwise, we will not establish a good relationship or a rapport with the patient and the therapy will not proceed forward.

In the model described in this book the author highlighted few features of the problem reality that should be fulfilled to create good change promoting problem frame. The incorrect pattern of behavior has to be well defined which means it has to have a need or a goal standing behind it well specified. There has to be well defined development line for the pattern, the beginning of it, the process itself and the end. The consequences have to be attached to the pattern. The problem has to be, when all these features are provided, defined in the solvable terms.

The definition of the problem has a crucial value to both the therapist and the patient. The patient can benefit from it in multiple ways, but the most important is that they can look at the problem from some different perspective, and thus reframe it in a way. This alone can bring a lot of change and new insight into the life of a patient. The therapist, if they create a clear defined reality for the problem, can observe the process of change within a patient and judge from their observations, on what level of change the patient is at the moment. This enables him or her to tailor the interventions to the specific patients.

Under all these observations there is, what the author calls, the constructivist principle. This principle states that we do not experience or go through real problems, but we rather experience some ideas, about the reality, that we do have. O'Hanlon (1990), for instance, expresses this idea in his paper in a following ways:

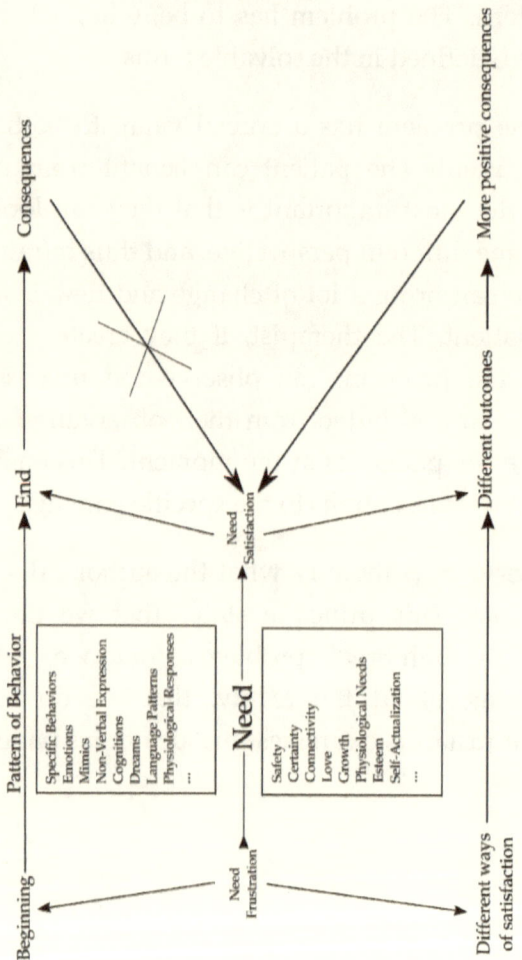

Figure 6: At the top part of figure 6 one can observe the structure of the problem. The behavioral pattern of some kind and of maladaptive nature, developed by the patient in order to satisfy a need of some sort, leads to consequences that provide discomfort of some sort rather than the satisfaction of the underlying need. The aim of Structural Pattern Reframing is to create, together with the patient, a reality for the problem that will generate new ways of satisfying the need. These new patterns, leading to more positive and adaptive consequences, provide the need satisfaction and comfort.

"(…) when clients have seen Gestalt therapists for more than few sessions, they usually have Gestalt-type problems and start to use Gestalt –like jargon. Likewise analytic therapists seem to engender analytic-type problems." (O'Hanlon, 1990, p.80)

"(…) we come with the idea that there is no way to discover what the real problem is in therapeutic situation. The therapist influences the data and the description in directions that are biased toward his or her theoretical model. (O'Hanlon, 1990, p.81)

If we assume that the following is true, we can come up with the statement, that the psychotherapeutic paradigms are nothing more or less, but the formulas for the preparation of the context for the problem a patient brings to the office. The therapist working with a patient can therefore, instead of putting themselves in a limited frame of one particular school of thought, choose between them, the best fitted one for the particular patient in a given situation. Even more, the therapist can combine cross – paradigmatically the ingredients of various schools, to create the best tailored reality for the resolution of the problem.

Another very important assumption that we can notice is that, if we treat the psychotherapeutic theory in an utilitarian fashion, we can outline some paradigms that are better and worst for the patient in terms of their healing process. The author, for example, claims that psychoanalysis can be pretty harmful to the patient and their work. It was Sigmund Freud himself (Freud, 1977) who postulated in his works, that when we start the therapy of a patient, we need to forewarn them, that the therapy will take years, the process will be hard and painful, and the patient may discover things about themselves that they may not like, not agree with and that may evoke hard feelings. That creates very difficult climate for a change to occur. It puts a patient in an overwhelming context, where every change, if it even occurs, will take huge amount of time and has to be followed by a very hard and painful work. It specifies the time parameter in years and the tempo of any change as very slow.

In fact, some results of psychoanalysis application supports the constructivist point described by the author. Elizabeth Loftus (1993), describes in her paper the cases of people who undergone psychoanalysis, which in consequence "reviled" suppressed memories of being molested or raped by parents, or being a witness of a murder . During the period of trails many times it came out that there was no evidence to support such charges or even the evidence was strongly against it. All of these may be considered a supporting argument for the thesis that the therapist in many ways influences the patient by choosing certain paradigm and secondly, it also shows how some theories can be counter change promoting and misleading. All this information is supposed to sensitize us even more on the importance of the way in which to create a good and well climate or context for a change to the patient.

Now, that we know the importance of the context in which we place the clients problem, we can ask another question: what are the main features of the reality that the therapist should take into consideration to create most change supporting reality?

In the research project described in this book, the author with his team noticed that almost all the analyzed cases of psychotherapy were based somehow on the concept of the pattern of behavior. This concept is well described in the first part of this book. Here, therefore, we only remind one more time that the pattern to be well defined has to have few features. First of all, the pattern has to lead the client to some goal or need. Many problems that people bring with them to the office are not defined at all, but are rather put into series of general statements or into the frame of clinical disorders. The frame of the pattern of behavior specifies for the patient what does not work correctly, and why he or she presents that kind of behavior. The need or a goal standing behind the pattern gives us and the patient the knowledge about why he or she does what he or she does.

To be more specific, if for example, a woman is angry at her husband each time he meets some other women, such a pattern satisfies a need of safety and may also satisfy the need for relation or intimacy. The husband over the course of time will reduce meetings with another people. The question is whether such a way of dealing with it is the best one? It may influence the quality of their relationship in a variety of ways. For example, it may harm the trust between them, or create a kind of bound based on fear or avoidance of the anger manifestations. If we define the need standing behind the pattern, we can encourage the patient to search for another ways of satisfying the need standing behind it, in other words, help him or her create more adaptive patterns of behavior, based on the new broaden out reality.

The pattern itself has to be also well defined for the patient and the therapist to know what they are dealing with. The pattern has to have a beginning, an end and something in between, the process. In other words, each human behavior is a response to something, so there is the need, which we already described, then somewhere the behavior starts, and then something happens until the need is satisfied, and after this, when it is satisfied well enough, the behavior ends. The therapist has to outline all this three ingredients, put the whole behavior in the context frame of the pattern. Otherwise we risk misunderstandings and, what is more important, if some of the key element will not be included within the pattern frame, the therapist may wrongly interpret the problem behavior, and he or she will deal with something which is not there.

Another situation which may occur is that, when one of the key features of the pattern will be left outside of the pattern frame. That may not necessary prevent patient and therapist to achieve some results together. Still, however, there is some part of the old behavior, which we left outside, so there is a risk that when a patient will display this part, it will bring the old pattern or ways of reacting back, and the effects of the treatment would not be long-lasting, since there is still some kind of behavioral or cognitive link to the past understandings and habitual sets.

Another important factor that we need to include into the reality are consequences of the old pattern of behavior. On some occasions, the consequences are in contradiction to the need that the pattern suppose to satisfy. Many times when we highlight the real consequences of some pattern of behavior, the patient somehow, through the ability to look at their problem from a different perspective, seems to come out with the conclusion, that it is not useful and that something else has to be done to live happier or healthier life.

Last thing is rather a general principle. The problem, that in consequence of the described frame will come out of incorrect patterns of behavior, has to be defined in a solvable terms. As presented in the chapter about the pattern of behavior, the definition of the problem based on the concept of a pattern, will in consequence bring to patients inner world multiple ways of resolution of the problem. When one suffers from some behaviors that all leads to a satisfaction of a need, then when one is familiarized with their pattern, the need behind it and consequences, one can create a lot of different ways of satisfying the same need. Patient needs to have a possibility, in other words, to change their behavior if they want in a way to create more satisfying way of dealing with a part of their reality. And they may achieve it by uncovering the need standing behind the pattern. The need, when introduced to the model, brings with it higher level of abstraction, introducing more ways or reaction. In simple words, it is easier to see different ways of satisfying a need than to find out how to change a specific behavior.

To summarize this part of the book, one is supposed to be aware that the aim of the first stage of the Structural Pattern Reframing Model is to put a behavior in a certain change promoting framework. The main tool to do this is a concept of a pattern of behavior provided by the author, but all other things presented in this part of the book also serve the same purpose. One can also use models of perspective shifting to support this process by changing the impact of patient's perspective on a problem. Lastly, given the idea of the constructivist principle, one can use whatever therapeutic, coaching or any other paradigm of thought to create a change-supporting environment. In doing this one should always have the good of the patient at first place, and not for example, the private preference of certain therapeutic school.

It is also important to mention that by putting the problem in a certain contextual framework, one already creates changes within the patients inner world by providing different understanding. By defining the features of the pattern, one reframes the problem and expands the possible solution repertoire. By using the dimensions presented in this chapter, the therapist may also show to the patient the additional dimensions of their problem. The dimensional model also provides us with some expansion of problem understanding by the patient and expansion of the possibilities of future actions. If there is a tendency within a patient to polarize the dimensional structure, or in other words, to be, for instance, more cognitive than emotional or more masculine than feminine, the possible course of the intervention may be to achieve the equilibrium in polarized dimensions. Lastly, the therapist may also utilize the patient's polarizations by recognizing them on this stage of intervention and then use it on further stages.

2. The preparation for the departure from the old pattern of behavior

After the first stage of the intervention, the client is left with a defined problem reframed into the new, more change promoting way. Still, however, it is an old pattern of behavior that we are dealing with. Such a pattern is at many occasions very well oiled habitual set that serves some purposes. To break such a pattern in the third step of the intervention, at first, we need to prepare a ground for such an operation. Otherwise we risk the evocation of resistant behavioral patterns that will protect the integrity of the subject and the reality that he or she knows and feels safe in. In the following section of the book the author discusses the importance and ways of weakening the impact strength of the old pattern of behavior. Only after we weaken such an impact it is safe to enter the third stage and lead the patient towards the pattern breaking process.

In the first stage of the intervention the therapist mainly asks some questions that enables to understand the problem situation. That stage is completed when the therapist puts the problem situation in a framework of a pattern of behavior which the client accepts. The clients acceptance is a key aspect here. It can be recognized by that the client works within the framework. Manifestations of such an acceptance enables us to proceed further.

The example below from the Anthony Robbins intervention (Robbins & Madanes, 2004b) shows the acceptance of a perspective shifting.

Lisa: In one way it is life threatening… it isn't …

Anthony Robbins: But it feels like it is ...

Lisa: It feels like it is (...)

A client, Lisa in this case, repeats the new, slightly altered interpretation of a bit of her inner reality, probably staying even unaware, that something was altered.

The same goes to all other parts of reality. If the patient does not resist the interpretation, we may assume that it is accepted. In case of larger parts of the reality, like for example, when we introduce the idea of the needs standing behind the pattern of behavior, we can observe the acceptance indirectly by the fact that the patient works within the framework. For example, he or she thinks of what needs he or she may satisfy by the pattern, and then generates the examples. That means that the patient works within this framework, and in consequence, he or she accepts it.

When the pattern of behavior is identified, the therapist can enter the second stage of the model. The aim of the second stage is mainly to diminish the impact of the old pattern of behavior on the reality of the patient. The aim of this is to gradate the process of change. If we impose on the patient's reality some new patterns or solutions too fast, it may evoke the resistance and in consequence be rejected. One of the main goals standing behind the second stage of the model is to diminish this tension by gradually departing from the old pattern of behavior. One can say, that this stage is designed in a way to depotenciate the resistance that may evoke due to the change within the patient that happened too fast.

The resistance in the process of change

The resistance as a therapeutic phenomenon was introduced to the field of psychotherapy by Sigmund Freud (Freud, 1977). He understood the resistance as a kind of inner unconscious process, that prevents some suppressed content to be pushed back into the conscious mind. The resistance in psychoanalysis is interesting even more due to its unconscious background. The patient entering the office has a certain readiness for the therapy, they want to change something in their life, they are willing to cooperate, but yet somehow the therapy does not proceed easily, and the therapist is stuck in some place. That kind of resistance may manifest in various ways, the client may not be able to recall something, or they are constantly speaking about the same thing. It may also manifest as an emotional dislike towards the therapist. In other cases patient will speak about a casual stuff, like job, or something that "just happened". Freud's (1977) idea on working with resistance was mainly to work on free associations, and to somehow walk it around. According to Messer (2002), the resistance serves the patient to express some of his inner elements, and to prevent some other from the expression. He also points out that it can be a healthy mechanism which helps assert the need for autonomy and separation from others.

Another perspective on the resistance that the author wants to refer shortly is a viewpoint presented by Milton H. Erickson (Erickson & Rossi, 1979). In this approach, the therapist accepts the patient's resistance and utilizes it to achieve the therapeutic change(Erickson & Rossi, 1979; Erickson, 1980a, 1980f). Let us consider an example illustrating that idea in practice. Once, a 12 year-old boy was sent to Dr Erickson by his parents with a bed-wetting problem(Erickson, 1980a). At the first session he resisted the therapist by stating that "he was tired enough to go to sleep" (Erickson, 1980a) and that he wants to go home. Erickson proposed that he could defeat the idea of an interview by going to sleep and not listening at all to what the psychiatrist has to say. A deep trance phenomena was established. Then Erickson performed a very complicated intervention, that the author would not be describing in details here, but the main principle in it was to farther utilize his resistance in combination with using various hypnotic techniques. Erickson, for example, stated that what the parents want from him is irrational (it was to stop the bed-wetting right away), and that he cannot do it because his body used all the energy on growth. It can only happen when the body will recover in some time. Then Erickson also claimed that it is impossible for the boy to stop the bed-wetting in a week, and that he would not be able to lose it completely even in two. The short description of this case study does not reflect all the subtle and complex ideas Dr Erickson involved in a process, but it clearly demonstrates completely different way of dealing with the resistance. In this approach the therapist accepts the resistance as a part of the problem, a part of communication, and he or she uses it to facilitate changes.

In the Structural Pattern Reframing, the resistance is also a pattern of behavior. We may, therefore, work with it as with any other pattern. It is, however, a pattern many times not directly connected to the problem itself, but to some other need like, for example, the need to feel safe. Many people stay in their old world for a long period of time, not because they like it, but because they are afraid of the new one. They are afraid of a change that may bring something better, but it also may not. The resistance may, as well, be affiliated with the need for autonomy or separation mentioned before(Messer, 2002). The therapist might choose to work with it like with any other pattern, but to avoid this, there is a second stage in the model, where the therapist weaken the impact of the old pattern of behavior, as well as its connections with the needs that it is supposed to satisfy.

The therapist may also choose to utilize the resistance to facilitate change within the pattern or to direct that activity towards the desirable changes or outcomes. Utilization of the resistance, as well as the utilization approach, will only be shortly discussed within this book as a part of the general attitude of the therapist in the therapeutic situation. A detailed discussion of this phenomena may be found for example in Erickson's *Hypnotherapy – An Exploratory Casebook* (Erickson & Rossi, 1979).

Going away from the old pattern

The ideas presented below are all focused on the ways a therapist may help the patient to weaken the impact of the old pattern of behavior on the patient's general overview of the situation. In some part this section of the book describes and develops further techniques and ideas presented in the previous chapter. It extends the ways we can work with them and presents ways of achieving goals of the second stage with them. Further some new ideas are also presented.

The introductory work with perspective

From the previous chapter we already know how to work with perspective. The reader was familiarized with the techniques of perspective shifting at the beginning of the model description because in the Structural Pattern Reframing Model the therapist uses the perspective shifting on all levels of the intervention. Each time we approach the problem reality some remains of the old pattern of behavior may evoke. The perspective shifting, both spiral and dimensional models, are very helpful in changing the power, impact and even the meaning of some behaviors and thoughts. In the first and the second stage of the intervention, the aim of the perspective shifting is to diminish the impact of the problem behavior and the negative sides of it, and to increase the meaning of the resources that one can use in a process of change.

It is very important to understand that to avoid the resistance, the patient has to figure out themselves that the old pattern of behavior is maladaptive to them and that a change would be with benefits for them. In other words, the question we ask here is how to operate with the perspective to prepare such an attitude within a patient?

First of all, the therapist has to do the basic work with the perspective which means, in a great shortcut, they have to diminish the range and power of negative sides and increase the power of positive sides of the patient's problem. One does this by paraphrasing and asking questions about the statements presented by the patient. One can use in this process the dimensional model of perspective shifting which helps the therapist identify the language patterns and then change them. For example, when the patient nominalizes the problem and speaks about it as if it were a thing (Bandler & Grinder, 1975), the therapist may want to bring it back to the process, bringing at the same time the responsible for the action back to the patient. In other words, patients very often when the therapy starts, use the labels like depression, fear, phobia, schizophrenia and so on. When the patient says:

"I have a phobia"

they, at the same time, put the process standing behind the phobia outside of their range of actions. They do have something, and do not do anything, as discussed above. The dimensional model gives us readymade solutions. One can change the nominalization into the process by asking the questions, for example, that would force the patient to think in terms of a process. In case of statements like: I have a depression or fear or anything else, the therapist may ask: what happens when you do that?

Another way to deal with the nominalizations is to ask the patient to demonstrate what exactly he or she does during the exemplary phobic situation, or depressive state. When patient performs the actions either in his imagination or by acting, the therapist paraphrases all the actions in such a way to underline the inner source of all actions. For example, the patient may report:

Patient: I feel an overwhelming fear.

Therapist: What feelings exactly do you evoke at the beginning of Your phobic reaction?

Patient: Well, first I feel the shivers

Therapist: where do You start your shivers in Your body?

Patient: well I do not know… In my legs at the beginning.

In such a way the therapist step by step puts the phobic process back into the patient. Then the therapist may change elements of phobic reactions with the patient and see what will be the difference, for example, using hypnosis as a tool to do so. By doing so, the therapist indirectly shows the patient different possibilities of response increasing their repertoire of reactions.

The therapist may also use the dimension global – local to change the impact of certain behaviors on the patient. For example, when the patient uses words like all the time, always and so on, which are in general global statements, the therapist may ask them, where and when exactly. The same refers to the situation where the time and place is not specified. For example, the patient who says:

"I have a depression"

does not specify where and when exactly it "happens" to them, so the therapist may ask, for example:

"when exactly do you feel depressed?"

It is important to highlight that this question does two things at the same time, it specifies the time when the patient feels depressed and it breaks down the nominalization. If they answer the question then they accept the reality where they do not have a depression but they feel depressed. It is a very important difference.

This brings us to a very important aspect of the language structure. Usually when the patient expresses somehow their ideas about the problem he or she suffers from, they will use many linguistic tricks in the descriptions. It is very unlikely that the therapist will face the problem where the nominalization will be the only thing to change. Most likely there will be multiple communication errors and distortions in any sentence the therapist will hear from the patient. The patient may have, for example, the linguistic pattern imprinted in which main features will be to globalize and nominalize the bad things that happened to them. The control over the things happening will be outside the subject and so on. On the other hand, the patient may simply, like in the Seligman description (Seligman, 2010) see everything bad as global, and they will be placing the responsibility for it in themselves, the same patient will do exact opposite in case of positive events. This pattern is mostly common in case of depressive patients. In the same time, they will see the depression as something outside of their control range and something overwhelming. The therapist in this stage has to make the patient think a bit differently. They must not tell the patient how he or she is supposed to think because such an approach will cause only the resistance and feeling of misunderstanding within the patient. The therapist acts here in an indirect fashion. He or she uses the perspective shifting models to make general statements more specific, to change the nominalization into process and to generally make the problem behavior less hard for the patient. The therapist applies these models in an indirect fashion, as stated above, which means they do not tell the patient what to do, or where to go, they just ask such questions that to be answered, it requires an inner change from the patient. Therapist may also use a paraphrase that will redirect slightly the way a patient sees their problem. A paraphrase used in such a way, just like a question, may contain changed statements. For example, if the patient states:

"I have a phobia"

the paraphrase that will change the nominalization to the process will be:

"Do You feel anxious from time to time?"

And another time, the paraphrase also attaches the time reference to the statement, making it less global.

In the same way one can use the Spiral Perspective Shifting model to attach the timeframes or, for example, switch between the levels of abstraction. A great instance of using the Spiral Perspective Shifting model lies in the Work of Byron Katie (Byron, 2008). Apart from doing a lot more in her interventions, she always asks four questions to her client's statement. The client generates a statement like, for example:

Patient: "I want my mom to be more responsible and take responsibility for her actions" (Byron, 2013).

Then the therapist, in this case it was Byron Katie, asks the first question:

"You want your mother to be more responsible, is that true?"

This question puts a problem statement into the bipolar framework where the patient has only two choices and can answer the question either with yes or with no answer. Another question is:

"Can You absolutely know that it is true?"

This question does a lot of things, it polarizes the statement, and it also can introduce some doubt. Can we really be absolutely sure that any statement we express is true? This is also the example of the spiral perspective shifting. The problem now shifts more towards the very strong statement. Such statements are then easier to discard because they do not allow any exceptions. In this exact presentation, the patient still claims that it is true, so Byron Katie decides to go even more in this way, by exaggerating the statement. She describes the mother who is very responsible with this words:

"You want her responsible, responsible, responsible. Is that a position that You really want to be left in?"

The patients answer is "no". And then, after a while, there comes another question:

"How do You react when You believe the thought "I want her to be more active?"

This question is a great example of the spiral perspective

shifting. Let us just analyze its structure for a moment.

"How do You react" – it is an example of putting the reference point back to the subject. It is the patient now who reacts on something and not someone else that causes something to the patient.

"When You believe the thought..." – here we can see that the perspective shifting took place. The perspective was raised two levels up to the more general level of abstraction. Such an operation, as we remember, results in a greater distance of the patient from the problem behavior.

"...The thought..." – is the first level. Now something is not a reality, it is a thought. The difference is vast. One can experiment with a thought, one can think it or not, and what is more important, it is the thought inside one's head that influences them, and not something from the outside, that the patient cannot control.

"...When You believe..." is another level. One can believe something or not, so it brings another possibility for the patient and it also reinforces the first perspective shifting from a reality to the thought.

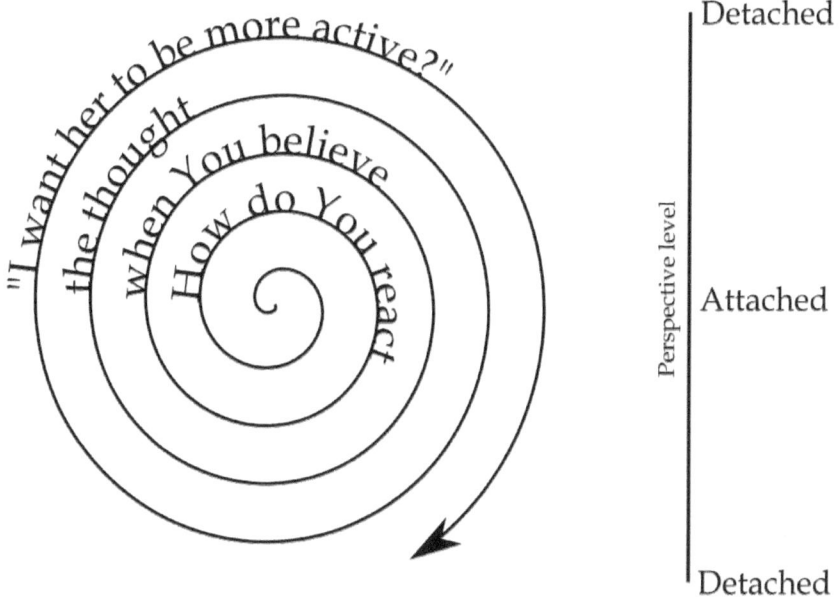

Detached

Attached

Detached

Perspective level

Figure 7: The Work of Byron Katie's question put into the framework of the spiral perspective shifting. By asking this question Byron Katie creates a perspective shift from more attached point of view to more detached, where the patient works with the thought rather than objective reality.

This is another way to decrease the force and power with which the old pattern of behavior influences the patient. The therapist can, at another levels of abstraction to it, make it more and more relative.

It is also important on this level of working with the perspective to seed new ideas into it. These ideas would become, in the next steps, the resources on which the therapist will build the change process. We can extend the patient's repertoire of behaviors by simply asking questions about alternative ways of behavior. That kind of questions have a structure like the following question from one of the Strategic Interventions of Anthony Robbins (Robbins & Madanes, 2004b):

"What would have happened if You had gone cry and gone crazy?"

If the patient accepts this question and answers it, the repertoire of his behaviors extends introducing some new possibilities of action.

Summarizing, the work with perspective continues from the first to the second level. The difference is that in the first step of the intervention the therapist uses the techniques of perspective shifting to build the basis for the new framework, and in the second stage he or she works more directly on change of specific aspects of the old reality to weaken its influence. At many occasions, but not always, the tendencies that make the old pattern have strong impact on the patient are the following:

The patient perceives the problem as global and talks about it in a global way. The therapist at this point reframes or changes that way of communicating into more local and specific.

The patient will be more cognitively oriented and thus prone to judgments. This closes him or her to different points of view and reinforces the old patterns. The therapist can associate the patient with the more emotionally oriented perception and enable them to experience the situation free from analysis and more nested in "now" than in the past and future.

The patient may create nominalizations for the processes. Therapist uses techniques to bring back to process into the place of nominalization. The result of it is that the patient takes more responsibility for their behaviors and is able to gain some more control on them.

Utilizing the patient's resources

Now, that we discussed the ways in which we use the perspective shifting to change the perception of the situation, we can discuss in short the idea of the resources in order to point out the importance of the positive reframing of the problem for the patient and their process of change.

The power of patient's resources is a very important thing to remember while working with someone. The concept of resources and its utilization was introduced to the therapy field by Milton H. Erickson(Erickson & Rossi, 1979), and was discussed in details in the first part of the book. Here, we will only refer to it shortly and discuss its role on this stage of intervention. Utilization Approach is described by Erickson (Erickson & Rossi, 1979) as certain way of thinking about the patient, in which the therapist do not impose upon the subject their authoritarian ideas, but rather he or she observes the ways in which the patient interacts, and behaves and then he or she utilizes these behaviors to facilitate trance or a change.

Now let us recall shortly what a resource is? What does a resourceful behavior mean? May we start this part of the chapter with a quote from Milton H. Erickson.

"All of us have a tremendous number of these generally unrecognized psychological and somatic learnings and conditionings, and it is the intelligent use of these that constitutes an effectual use of hypnosis" (Erickson, 1980d)

This sentence in part explains to us what Doctor Erickson understands as a resource. A resource can be any behavior or learning that, if wisely used, can facilitate a change. One can say that if we look in this way on the patient and their problem behavior, everything may become a resource in a process of a change. One has to have a certain optimism while looking at the patient to see their good sides and possibilities to utilize their behaviors (Walters & Havens, 1994).

In Structural Pattern Reframing Model, a resource can be anything. There are, however, two kinds of resources outlined useful at this stage of the intervention. First kind is a direct resource and second is an associational resource.

The first one is something that comes directly from the situation. It may be a part of a problem behavior or any other behavior that occurred at the time of the intervention or is a part of the pattern of behavior. That kind of behavior may become a powerful resource when the meaning of it will be changed through the process of reinterpretation or reframing into the manifestation of something positively valued.

Let us consider the problem of stubbornness, for example, as a kind of direct resource. A problem like stubbornness can, if well reframed, be perceived as patience and persistence. And these qualities can be then used to facilitate a change. Direct resource are also all the good qualities that a patient displays within a session. For example, a woman can be jealous and dominant but, on some occasions during the session, she displays the examples of care and feminine fragility. At the same token, a depressive patient many times is able to display some sort of humor or irony (Beck et al., 1979). The therapist's task is to outline all this kind of manifestations and build upon them a resourceful states. Many times people do have a certain tendency to see, for instance, negative qualities in themselves and others (Beck et al., 1979). This causes them to omit, many times not consciously, positive qualities that are displayed at the same times. Outlying these qualities, and noticing them, makes them more available for the patients conscious attention (Zeig, 1990). It also diminishes the power of the negative associations by, in a way, balancing the neural associational network with positive associations activation. It is important to remember that our goal in evoking the resources is not to impose them by force on the patient, and it is not to convince them of it, but rather to just mark it and highlight without any comment or discussion. By positive reframing of the behaviors and utilizing them for the future change, we weaken the connection between these behaviors and the old pattern of interpretation. We also change the view of the patient on the case and enrich it with more positive associations.

The other type of resources are those of the associational nature. These are all the resources that are evoked by doing some procedure and not directly derived from the situation. A great example of that kind of resources are the Early Learning Sets (Erickson et al., 1976; Zeig, 1980b), that were, for example, evoked by Erickson through performing a regression to the early age on the patient. A regression itself is a good example of such a technique through which the therapist reaches some past events in search for resources, like curiosity, feeling of safety, open-mindedness and so on, to then activate them and associate them with the current situation.

One of the aims in the second stage is to change the meaning of the elements of the problem reality in such a way so that the patient will want to change the behavior themselves. The therapist may achieve this by using the reframing and change meaning techniques, as well as underlying the positive intentions standing behind the pattern of behavior. The patient is jealous because he or she cares for his or her partner. This care is a positive reinterpretation and a resource. In further stages one can use this resource in creating new patterns of behavior by finding new, better ways of satisfying these needs.

The creation of a new frame of reference

Another very important goal of the second stage of the Structural Pattern Reframing Model is a creation of the new frame of reference. Albert Einstein included in his Relativity Theory the idea that:

"(The space coordinates and time)... are relative as much as they depend on a state of the chosen inertial system ." (Einstein, 2001 p. 91)

The inertial system is a relatively static system of referential points, in which we place the space coordinates and time. That kind of explanation is a great oversimplification but it illustrates one of the key features of the Structural – Constructive Approach proposed by the author. O'Hanlon develops similar idea in his paper: *A Grand Unified Theory for Brief Therapy: Putting Problems in Context* (O'Hanlon, 1990). According to him, the therapist recreates the problem situation in a way by putting it into a therapeutic context. The patients attempting the therapy in certain modality, like for example Gestalt, Psychoanalytic or for instance Cognitive – Behavioral approaches, after few sessions put their problems in a certain referential frame, connected with the approach. In consequence their problems suddenly adjust its dynamics to applied approach. The conclusion of it is that if the same patient in few parallel realities chooses different oriented therapist, he will go through the process of healing or change in a totally different way, and length of time.

Being aware of this constructive role of the paradigm or school of therapy, the therapist can consciously create the reality of a problem in a way to promote the change. The role of the new frame of reference in stage two of the Structural Pattern Reframing is to enable patient to absorb a new point of view on his or her problem that will activate the motivation and processes responsible for the change in the patterns of behavior.

New frame of reference is not a new pattern of behavior. It is rather a context, an Einstein's inertial system, in which the patient, as well as the therapist, may understand the problem and see its dynamics. In Structural Pattern Reframing, the main concept, around which the therapist builds their intervention, is a pattern of behavior, previously described in the first section of this book. For a short recollection, one needs to remember that the pattern is not the same as an observable behavior, a basic unit of analysis in behavioral approaches(Skinner, 1976; Watson, 1919, 1930). The pattern of behavior can be a set of behaviors, both observable and not observable. It may include the emotional responses, verbal and non-verbal communication, certain behaviors and responses, and many more. One can call some set of elements a pattern when it is recurring and it serves certain need or a goal or a set of these. The new frame of reference proposed here puts the problem behavior in a context of a pattern of behavior. As we remember from the previous chapters, the main features of the pattern of behavior are for it, it would have a beginning, and end points specified, as well as the need standing behind it. Another thing is the behavioral set that leads us from the beginning to the end point and is directed towards the satisfaction of a particular need or set of needs.

Such a construction of the therapeutic context provides the therapist and the patient with another important feature - to define the problem in a solvable terms. If a patient comes to the office and says "I have depression", they not only come with a label that makes them believe that something is outside of their range of control, and that it is overwhelming, but they also do not know what to do, and how to solve their problem, because in its definition there is no solution for it. If the therapist follows the directions presented in this book, they are able to redefine the problem in a solvable way. In a problem behavioral pattern there is a result of something behind it, a need or a goal, then there are multiple other ways of satisfaction for this need or a goal. So right away they create the reality for a problem in which they provide the alternative ways of action.

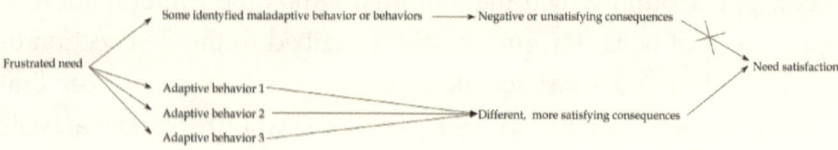

Figure 8: The standard frame of reference with typical components. The maladaptive pattern with its consequences is presented and defined. It is presented how it does not satisfy the need standing behind it. The need standing behind the pattern is also defined. The need generates in consequence, as higher order function more than one possibility of the satisfaction. Based on the need the therapist together with the patient create new alternative, more adaptive patterns of behavior, leading to different consequences and need satisfaction.

Almost all of this features one can find in the chapter about the pattern of behavior itself. It is, therefore, important to point out the difference between the pattern of behavior and the frame of reference, though it is not the same thing. The pattern of behavior is a unit of analysis, it is something a therapist looks for in the whole problem reality. In the Structural-Constructive approach the therapist looks for the patterns in behavior. The way in which one presents the problem to the patient is the frame of reference. In the chapter above, the suggested frame of reference includes the pattern as well as the needs standing behind it as an integral part. The therapist may, however, chose to work on an indirect level and attempt to break the pattern and introduce new one into the framework of the patient, for example, in a more Ericksonian way or by paradoxical assignments. Then, the therapist, for instance, may use the concept of the pattern to design the activity that will enable the patient, in an indirect manner, to experience the problem in a different way (Weeks & L'Abate, 1982), thus causing the pattern to break and be replaced in action by some different experience.

In this way the therapist may utilize the pattern of behavior to create the change promoting frame of reference, but they may choose not to do it, and still use the pattern of behavior as a main unit of their therapeutic intervention. It means that they may still design the assignment or the intervention based on the principles derived from the pattern idea, and not mention about it at all.

In other words, to make the distinctions even more clear in the first stage, the therapist uses the pattern of behavior as a tool to diagnose the dynamics of the problem. They look for the information necessary to create any intervention based on the idea of the pattern. This process in part also creates a basic frame of reference for the problem, but on this stage it is not the main goal. It, in a way, happens on its own, in the process of information gathering and structuring. In the second stage, the therapist introduces the frame of reference in a planned way. They may do it in a way proposed above using the pattern of behavior, or may choose from many other ideas, but do it in a conscious, planned and structured way.

The establishment of the departure from the old pattern of behavior

The establishment of the departure from the old pattern of behavior is an important part of the second step of the Structural Pattern Reframing Model. It is the moment when the patient starts to see the other side of the pattern. When he or she starts to notice the need for a change of some sort. It is a kind of readiness for a change. It does not mean that the change will occur, but rather that if the patient is properly directed and stimulated, he or she can implement some changes into his or her life.

To achieve this readiness, one has to wisely work with perspective in which the patient seize their problem. Another, very important thing to achieve during this state, is to reframe the problem in positive and solvable terms. It is very important to define the problem in solvable terms so that people would be able to see some possible ways of alternative actions. If the therapist defines the problem reality in terms of the pattern, with all its ingredients well defined, the assumption of multiple ways of action is fulfilled. But there is another very important assumption in the model. The problem has to be defined in a positive way. It means that it has to be perceived on this stage by a patient as some positive movement in their lives. The idea of a pattern partly fulfills this assumption. For instance, if we define the problem between two partners as the problem with jealousy, then we will find the needs standing behind it, almost always it will be defined in a positive way. In case of jealousy the possible needs can be, for example, on a side of a woman, a need for safety, or need for love. If one defines the problem as a pattern of behavior, that was meant to lead to a satisfaction of a need for love, that is a positive reinterpretation. If one accepts this interpretation, it is almost certain that he or she would like to look for more satisfying ways to fulfill this need. Of course, in case of marital problems, the situation is almost always a bit more complicated, and there is an interaction of more than one pattern of behavior, from both partners.

For example, the author of this paper, once met a couple, a man and a woman, who were dealing with the problem of jealousy. The wife was always very jealous when the husband was going out with friends in the evening. At first, she was not manifesting it, but after some time, she started to get angry at him and as a result they were quarreling more and more. Then, the husband started to isolate from the wife and as a result, she started to be even more aggressive. This example illustrates the simple interaction of two patterns of behavior that, in result, amplified one another. The woman has a family background for her fear, her father left her and her mother when she was a small girl. She probably was in a way unconsciously afraid that she would lose her husband. The pattern was reestablished with the new interpretation where the wife was trying to gain love and safety from the husband, the husband created the pattern of departure to fulfill the need for independence. The patients were then able to see their conflict as a result of a certain way of fulfilling the needs for love and safety on a part of a woman and the need for self-determination, on the husband's side. An important thing is that they loved each other and had no idea why it all happened this way. They both felt misunderstood and misinterpreted. When the new interpretation appeared, they immediately saw a need for a change. The wife did not want to limit her husband contacts with friends, and he did not want her to feel unsafe or threatened. The pattern of a wife was also linked with her childhood experience so that the husband could see the brother context, as well as for him not to feel guilty for the situation. As a result, they were able to enter the third stage and break the old pattern of behavior by assuming that it fulfilled neither his nor her needs. In consequence, new patterns of expression were established, and so they now are able to communicate better, with more understanding, as well as they spend more time together, both alone and with friends.

This, however, would not be possible if the author did not redefine the situation in a positive way. If the couple had not experienced this change, it is very possible that they would have used the ideas created within the course of therapy to go even deeper into conflicts. Positive reframing prevents that from happening.

Last thing that the therapist is supposed to do is to highlight the consequences of the old pattern. It is very important to show where the old pattern of behavior goes to, and that it does not satisfy the needs that it was designed for. In case of the intervention addressed in short above, the consequences of the pattern of the wife were growing detachment of the husband. So one may say, that the result of the old pattern of behavior was totally opposite to what it was designed for. This fact was a powerful motivation for both partners to change the way they interacted.

These consequences are supposed to naturally derive from the pattern and, as any other things, they should be accepted by the client or a patient. These consequences are one of the key features in the process of change, next to the needs on which the therapist bases the change process. It is the feeling that these consequences bring up within the patient when they realize that their previous actions did not serve their goals and their own interest or well-being.

3. Breaking the old pattern

Breaking the old pattern of behavior is the most difficult part of the whole intervention. It is the moment where the old set of behaviors are no longer accepted by the patient. The need and readiness for a change appears.

At the beginning, it is important to note that there are many patients that are unable to break their patterns of behavior on their own, even with the therapist's help. It happens many times when the pattern is of unconscious nature like, for example, in case of sleep disorders, many obsessive-compulsive behaviors and so on. In such cases one needs to break the pattern on the unconscious level. The ways of working with the pattern on the unconscious levels will be described in the second volume of this series.

The idea of breaking the pattern

The consequence of the accomplishment of the second stage requirements is the readiness of the patient to question the old pattern of behavior. Generally speaking, a pattern of behavior is a more or less complex way of dealing with some difficulty created by the patient. That pattern, whatever it is, brings the patient a relief or a solution of some kind of dilemma. The only problem with the pattern is, that it does not deal with the problem in an ecological way. It means that it, at the same time when dealing with the problem, harms a patient or their surroundings in some way. The patient, however, due to the benefits that they have by applying the pattern, will attach to it. In other words, the pattern is reinforced by the benefits a person derives from. Therefore, it is almost impossible to impose on patient some kind of new understanding right away, and such an approach will in consequence evoke a huge amount of both conscious and unconscious resistance. In other way, the patient will always protect their way of thinking. Therefore, the Structural Pattern Reframing Model deals with that problem by gradually walking the patient through the perspective change during which they are able to perceive the pattern in a different way, and find out by themselves that it is a good idea to change it.

Milton H. Erickson noticed and pointed this problem out in a following way:

"No two people necessarily have the same ideas, but all people will defend their ideas whether they are psychotically based or culturally based or nationally based or personally based. When you understand how man really defends his intellectual ideas and how emotional he gets about it, you should realize that the first thing in psychotherapy is not to try to compel him to change his ideation; rather, you go along with it and change it in a gradual fashion and create solutions wherein he himself willingly changes his thinking." (Zeig, 1980a) p. 335

This idea of graduation and of the patient's independence in discovering and reaching new understandings must be a core of this stage interventions. The therapist does not break the old pattern of behavior, he or she rather leads a patient to new understandings and new contexts, so the patient him or herself come up with the conclusion that there is something that has to be changed. The previous stages put a patient in a new context and weaken the link between the old pattern and the emotional and cognitive responses of the patient. The aim of this stage is to make the patient accept the reality in which the old pattern of behavior did not fulfill its basic intention or the need standing behind it. The result of this stage is supposed to be the new attitude of the patient towards change. He or she has to see the need for a change and has to be willing to do it. The framework of the pattern will then automatically provide new solutions in the fourth stage of the intervention.

Now, we will discuss in short how the therapist can achieve this goals by using few simple frameworks.

Working with the positive intentions

No matter what the therapist does, he or she must remember the importance of reframing the problem in such a way so that it would reflect some of the positive intentions of the subject. One of the most important tendencies in human self-image is to perceive oneself as a good and successful person(Greenwald, 1980). Therefore, it is important to work with the positive intentions. If the patient feels criticized, they may evoke the resistance towards the therapy or just leave the therapy in favor of protecting their own inner world and its integrity. The model based on the needs or goals provides us with a simple way of positive reframing. Therapists may define the behavior as a pattern of some kind which fulfills some kind of need. In this way, we always provide patient with the definition of some behavioral tendency towards something good rather than with the description of their deficits, like in the causal psychotherapy. Another thing that the author observed is that, it is useful also to underline some successes that the patient achieved even though he or she was using the old pattern. This prevents the patient from falling into guilt or sadness caused by a new view point on the old pattern of behavior.

When the therapist puts a pattern into a new frame of positive intentions, another step is to outline once more where exactly the pattern does not fulfill the needs standing behind it. Usually the pattern does some work towards the fulfillment of some goal or need, but it does not do it in the most efficient way. So, after the outline of where it does and what good comes out of this, the therapist can proceed to the point where he or she shows the patient where it does not work and why. To do it, he or she has to work on the same needs or goals as previously. It is crucial because these goals and needs were accepted by the patient and came out of him. They also have to be important needs for the client, the ones that s/he will be identifying themselves with. Using the needs we show to the patient where the pattern does not fulfill them. The therapist may do it, as a form of some kind of summary, when they gather all the things said before in the course of intervention and, in this framework, they will present to the patient the consequences of the pattern that does not fit the need standing behind it. For example, when a mother develops a fear for her children because she is afraid that something may happen to them when they are outside (and outside of her control zone), she does it because she loves her children and wants to protect them. So, important values in this particular problem are safety, love and care for children. The positive aspect of this pattern is that probably her children seem safe. Another positive is that one can see the real love coming out of this behavior. On the other hand, such an isolation and too much care may harm children in terms of their independence and ability to cope with difficulties, to name only two consequences for the purpose of this chapter. No loving mother would like her children to be like this. This is an example of underlying the positive intentions and results and then showing the places in which the pattern contradicts with them. The therapist may also show to the patient at this point more consequences. He or she may build up how the pattern will affect the children in the future and how they may replicate it. Such a framework will have a motivational impact on the patient and will reinforce the belief that the old pattern is an incorrect or ineffective one.

Detachment of the pattern from the needs

Another important step in this stage of the intervention is a detachment of the incorrect pattern from the needs that it is supposed to fulfill.

In general, the whole process of intervention till this moment serves this purpose. The therapist works with the view point of the patient, decreases the amount of overgeneralizations, works with perspective, reframes the meaning of the behaviors, then he or she creates a new context for the old pattern so that the patient could come into a conclusion that this is not the best possible choice of behavior in a given moment and time. What the client should have achieved till this moment is an understanding of a problem in a new framework and an acceptance of this. In consequence the client should have the readiness and should feel the need to change something. Such a state is not equal with a change because the client does not have to know what he or she has to do in a different way. It is rather a readiness for some change, a readiness to do some work in favor for a change. The detachment of the pattern from the needs is a tipping point in this process. It is like a declaration of some sort that the client is ready for a change. That is why it is so important to go through it and underline it.

In this step the therapist follows the patient in a process of understanding that the pattern does not fulfill the needs it is supposed to. The therapist may do it by providing the examples of this mismatch. The therapist may also create a vision of a future, with the consequences derived from the pattern on the life of a patient and his surroundings. Many times the vision, provided by a therapist, in which the patient can see the consequences of his pattern of behavior on his family, children, and so on, creates high motivation within the patient towards some change.

The interpretation the therapist creates with the patient has to clearly show that the needs that stand behind the pattern are not fulfilled by it. The interpretation is supposed to indicate some other goals and needs that a patient does fulfill with this pattern, and that are in contradiction with his most valued goals. In other words, the main task in this step is to show to the patient that their behavior does some opposite thing than the one they wanted to obtain.

An example of such a reinterpretation can be viewed in Anthony Robbins intervention with a patient called Jim (Robbins & Madanes, 2004a). Jim was a man in his middle years, and an owner of a big company. The time he visited one of Anthony Robbins seminars, he was at the point where he lost everything, his money and company he owned was gone. Not only did he lose his own assets but also his costumers and friends lifesavings. He was also at the point where he was thinking of a suicide as a solution to at least some of his problems. He had a life policy that he thought would secure financially his wife if he eventually passed away. Anthony Robbins noticed that the dominant characteristic of Jim was that he was caring for people around him. Then Robbins built this feature up by encouraging Jim to provide more examples. Then he reframed the suicide as a selfish act, that in consequence will only make things worse. If Jim did it, his wife would lose him forever, and she would never forgive herself that she was not able to prove him that there is so much more than money, that counts for her. Consequences and arguments like these were provided to reframe the suicidal pattern in such a way, so that it would be in a contradiction with the need that it was supposed to fulfill. This is an example of the process of detachment of the old pattern from the needs it was supposed to fulfill in the past. The therapist reframes the situation in such a way so that the behavior no longer looks adequate to the situation. Moreover, it works against the main goals of the situation.

Many times when the therapist provides reinterpretations in such a fashion, the patient may provide another examples supporting the thesis that the pattern of behavior really does what it is supposed to. In such a case, the therapist reframes provided examples in the same way to show the inadequacy of patterns standing behind them. If the resistance occurs, the endeavors of a patient towards protection of the old patterns are too strong, that may indicate that there has to be some additional work done on the previous stages of the intervention.

General procedure of pattern detachment – summary

The first thing the therapist is supposed to do is to put the pattern of behavior into some kind of framework that will enable the process of reinterpretation. In the model of Structural Pattern Reframing the author suggests that it may be the framework of human needs provided by Robbins (Robbins, 2007), or the one provided by Maslov in his pyramid model (Maslov, 1943, 2009). It can be any other model as well that will provide the possibility of further reframing. The identification of the needs standing behind the pattern gives the patient a broader point of view, which in consequence puts the patient and the therapist on more general level in terms of the spiral reframing model. The more general viewpoint gives to the therapist the possibility of introducing the new interpretation. In other words, if we would consider a given behavioral pattern, we can clearly see that it leads to a satisfaction of some needs or goals. On this level this is everything we can identify. There are only few possibilities of some meaning change in such a situation. When we would shift the level up, to a more general one, in this case the level of needs, when the lower level, the level of exact pattern becomes only one of many ways of satisfaction of a given need or a goal.

Another step on this stage of the intervention is to turn the needs against the pattern. The therapist may do it using various techniques from, for example, Cognitive Behavior currents(Beck et al., 1985, 1979; Maxie C Maultsby, 1984). The main goal is to create such an interpretation of a behavioral pattern, so that it no longer fulfills the need standing behind it. Moreover, the interpretation is supposed to be built in such a way so that the pattern would cause the needs to be even more frustrated than when the pattern is not applied. Anthony Robbins' example was given right above (Robbins & Madanes, 2004a).

To clarify the subject more, let us think of another example, the example of jealousy. First, the therapist is supposed to think in terms of what kind of positive needs that kind of pattern should fulfill. One can go with the patient through the needs such as a need for love, intimacy, safety, certainty, self-esteem and so on. When the therapist established the framework with the needs in it, he can then turn the needs against the pattern. Let us say, for example, that the needs standing behind the pattern are the need for intimacy and safety as well as love. The patient wants to spend more time with his or her partner and he or she wants to feel more loved which in consequence would make him or her feel more safe. If the patient accepts such an interpretation, then the next step is to create a framework when the pattern contradicts the needs standing behind it. In this example the therapist may develop the vision of future consequences when the jealous behaviors really do not bring the patient and the partner together but only create more detachment. For example, the patient is more and more jealous and in consequence his or her partner isolates from him or her more and more, because he or she feels dominated and forced to do things, and this may evoke the behavioral pattern that will be focused on a goal of bringing back some freedom and independence.

To make such an interpretation stronger in its influence the therapist then may develop it by providing examples from the life of the patient. In an ideal situation we encourage the patient to develop some examples. The moment the patient creates the example of such a behavior and its consequences is the moment when he or she accepts and develops on his or her own the new framework for the pattern of behavior. Then, the final step is to observe and, if necessary, to acquire the acceptance of the new framework by the patient. When this is done we will be able to go into the next stage of the structural intervention.

4. Introducing the new pattern of behavior

In the end of stage three, the therapist achieved the following in working with the patient:

- The perspective of the patient on the pattern of behavior is altered

- The pattern is reframed into the context of a new framework (for example needs models)

- The pattern is detached from the needs, which in consequence changes the patients viewpoint on the pattern

- There is a readiness within a patient to commit a change

With all this points covered, one can set about creating the new pattern of behavior. In fact, the process of creating new associations and ideas within a patient started long ago, and develops through all the stages of the structural intervention. In stage four, the therapist, however, focuses directly on creating more adjusted pattern for the patient. The passing from the stage three to stage four is supposed to be a natural and automatic process. It is a natural occurrence that when one disqualifies one way of functioning, working or doing something, it is necessary to create or provide another. When the therapist accomplishes the third stage of the intervention, there is a gap, an empty space that is created by the absence of the old pattern of behavior, that was there previously, and was declassified by the patient in the process of an intervention. It is one of the most important things in the structural model to provide new understandings and new framework that will generate different behavior. If the patient is left alone in this stage of the intervention they will most likely go back to the old, well-known, habitual pattern of behavior. Many times when the therapeutic process occurs, the therapist is able to create a situation together with the patient, where they start being aware of the inadequacy of the old ways of functioning, and then the patient is left with this, due to theoretical assumptions, that for example, there is no time yet for the behavioral changes, or that the patient is supposed to discover all the things on their own. The result of such an attitude is the return of the patient to the old pattern of behavior and their frustration, due to the fact, that he or she starts being aware that what he does is not what he wants, but he cannot find a way to act in a different way. It is, therefore, important to help them find a new way. It does not mean that the therapist should impose on patient some arbitrary ways and patterns of behavior. It does not mean that patient at this stage accepts and seeks for readymade easy solutions that the therapist is supposed to generate right away. On this stage, when the gap occurs, the patient needs guidance. The therapist is a bit like a companion in a journey. In this journey they walk together with the patient and highlight some things, point out what the patient also observes on some stages during the journey. Below, we would try to investigate more deeply the structure of this journey and the role of the companion that the therapist should fit himself into.

Creating new framework

In general, creating new pattern of behavior means to create the new framework for the problem that will itself generate new ideas and behaviors, from which the patient will be able to choose and exercise new behavioral repertoire. The important start point is the attitude towards the old pattern of behavior created in the previous stages. The old pattern does not meet the needs it is supposed to satisfy. Moreover, it is in conflict with these needs. The new pattern of behavior, therefore, is supposed to be based on the same needs. First step of the process of building the new frame of reference is to create a new identity for the patient in which their goals are clearly highlighted, put into the frame of positive intentions. Then, working with this identity, the therapist creates the framework based on constructs like, for example, human needs in which the old behaviors can be viewed from the new perspective of the new pattern and new identity. Then, in the end, the patient and the therapist explore the new possibilities of behavior derived from the new framework. In the end, the therapist closes up all the old patterned behaviors of the patient and his surroundings in the new interpretation. After this process is completed, one more time, patient and the therapist explore new possibilities. Below, we will now analyze more deeply all the stages of this process named here.

Working with Resources

First thing, that the therapist should keep in mind is to maintain an open resource-driven attitude. From the chapter of this book on utilization approach in the first section, the reader may already be familiar with the meaning of this statement. In general, on this stage of the intervention one has to reframe the experiences of the subject in such a way, so that a new possibilities of behavior emerge from it. The jealousy, for instance, if reframed into the unsatisfied need for love, does bring some more opportunities of action. Any behavior or attitude may be reframed and thus seen as a resource important for the process of change that is just emerging.

Creating the new identity

The idea of creating the new identity was observed and mainly used by Anthony Robbins in his Strategic Intervention approach (Robbins & Madanes, 2004a, 2004b). It is believed by the author of this book that it is a valuable tool in working with many kinds of problems. In many cultures people give themselves or receive new names in a process of some kind of initiation on another step in life. The moment of passing from one place to another, from childhood to adulthood, for instance, is marked by receiving a new name in many religions and cultures. At the same token, the woman usually changes the surname while entering the marriage. Many important events connected with some changes are in our society marked by additional name or the name change. In the process of change in the Structural Pattern Reframing model, the therapist helps the client change the meaning of some behaviors and situations in order to generate more possibilities of action. It also helps the client take more responsibility for their lives and actions. All these changes put people in a situation, in which new understandings, viewpoints and possible choices are emerging. Thus, we can suspect that all this novelty may evoke confusion, some doubts, also some enthusiasm, and many more feelings and emotions. With all this, a person him/herself will also change in a way, as a general system. That is why it is important somehow to mark these changes, and prepare the subject for it. Giving a name to the new identity, which the therapist co-creates with the client, is one of the ways. Like in many other change situations, giving a name or changing the name of a subject is a natural culturally based process. It helps a subject reorient, marks the point in time when the change occurred or started to occur.

In the structural model, the author proposes to introduce the new name or a nickname during stage four of the intervention, when the patient is able to work within the reframed framework and can process the information in a new positive and more change promoting way - in other words, when the reality of the new pattern of behavior and new framework is established. The nickname twines together and connects these exact changes in a form of a new identity, creating something with what a patient could identify him/herself.

The therapist introduces the concept of a nickname simply by asking the patient about it. Therapist may ask, for example:

How will we name the new You?

What will a new name/nickname of the real You be you are about to become?

One can also use the powerful and resourceful process of regression to the stage of early childhood, or early learning set (Erickson et al., 1976; Erickson & Rossi, 1979), and thus ask a question like:

How did people who love You call You in the childhood?

It is, however, advised to check in advance if the patient has a kind of pleasant childhood memories that could connect the new identity with the nickname. There is always a risk in bringing back some traumatic experiences while evoking the childhood memories, that is why it is important to know in advance that there is a resource we can utilize in this period. On the first stages of the intervention, when the therapist gathers the information about the pattern, as well as reframes the first aspects of the general framework, they usually check the childhood in search for the genesis of the pattern and eventual resources. Now, in stage four, one can utilize some of these information to amplify the process of positive change.

Working on the constructs (needs)

As previously mentioned, the whole structural intervention is based on creating a framework, for the past and future behaviors. That framework provides the patient with a new perspective, through which s\ he can see his or her behaviors in a new change promoting light. The work based on constructs done on earlier stages of the intervention deals with the following processes:

-   The problem is already defined in terms of needs or any other framework that enlarges the amount of possibilities and repertoire of behaviors.

-   The unsatisfied needs are defined (reframing is done).

-   The negation of the old pattern adequacy is accomplished by the patient together with the therapist

-   The readiness for some new input is established

On this stage, the aim of working with the constructs is to provide a patient with the new framework or the new interpretation of his or her behaviors. This interpretation is supposed to suggest some new ways of acting. In this book it is advised to work with the concept of human needs (Maslov, 1943,

2009; Robbins, 2007), due to its structure. The need is a concept from the higher, more general level of abstraction than the pattern of behavior. Due to this fact, if the therapist puts a behavior into a framework of needs, he or she puts it, at the same time, at a different, more abstract and more general level. The result of this is that it generates more possibilities. For example, if someone's pattern of behavior includes jealousy, like in the case discussed throughout the book, the therapist may choose to work on the level of jealousy, but they may choose the model of work presented here, and try to identify the needs standing behind the pattern.

Previously, it was assumed that, for example, the needs for love and safety may be involved in such a pattern. Now, the therapist has everything they need to create the new framework for the pattern. In fact, the framework has already been seeded (Zeig, 1990) or primed in the moment when the therapist introduced the need construct and built the entire problem on this construct. This endeavor reorients the problem in a different direction. It already introduces more possibilities, even before it is even mentioned.

On this level, when the old pattern has already been rejected by the patient as dysfunctional, the question the therapist is supposed to answer with the patient is the following:

How can we satisfy the needs we outlined before in a more adaptive way?

On this stage, the therapist, using the framework of needs, follows the patient and supports him or her in discovering new ways of acting and behaving. For example, if a woman wants her partner to be closer to her, and now she knows already that using the jealousy pattern she obtains opposite results, she may want to consider different ways of behavior. The therapist may directly suggest some behaviors, like spending some more time together doing some activity which will involve both of them. The therapist may also just ask a patient for some new ideas that come to their mind. The new framework should work in such a way within a patient to enable some new ideas.

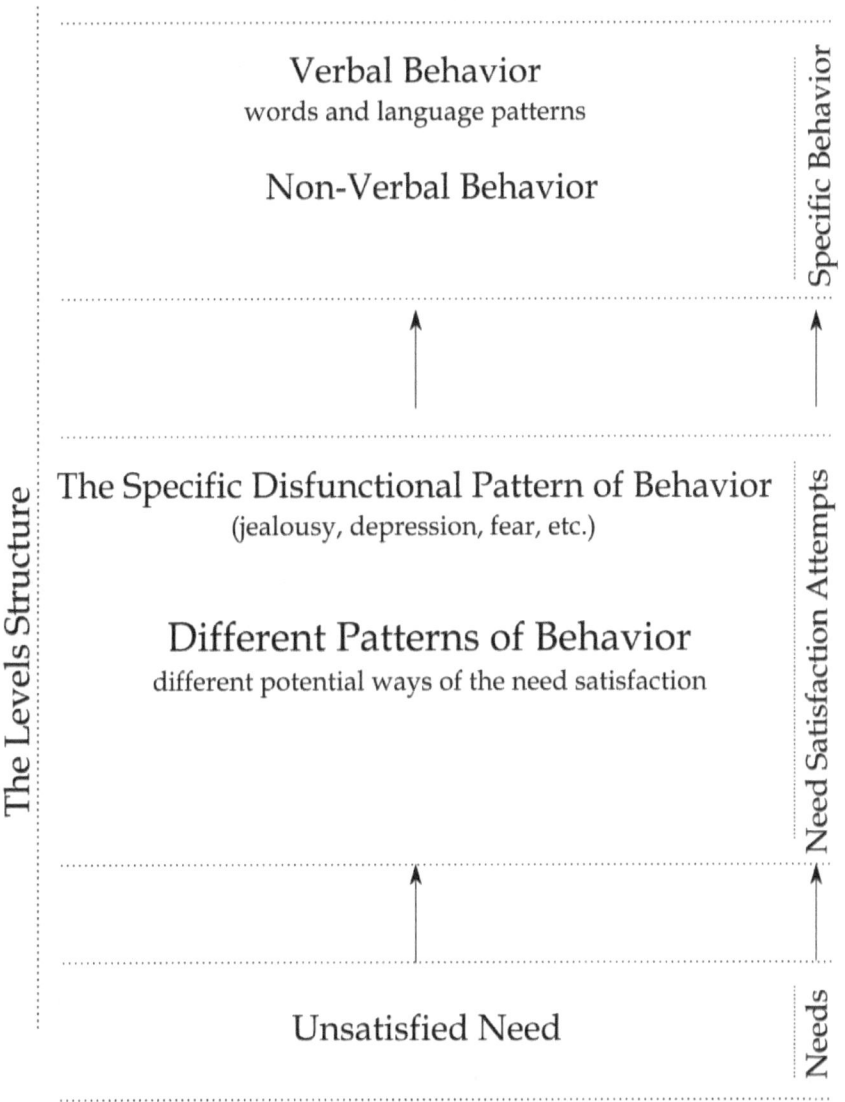

Figure 9: The level structure of the Structural Pattern Reframing conceptual framework. The first most general level is a level of needs. The unsatisfied need leads us to more specific level of Need Satisfaction Attempts. When a patient develops a specific way of the behavioral pattern they may fix their attention on specific way of satisfying the need. In such a

case, they may have difficulties with the change in the attitude, due to the fact that they will not see other possibilities. Particular behavioral pattern manifests itself on even more specific level of Specific Behaviors. When patient fixes on this level, they can feel the discomfort, but are unaware of what is the source of the problem. To bring back the awareness, the therapist defines the pattern (goes up the level structure towards more general levels). To enable a patient to generate different more adaptive solutions, a therapist defines the problem in terms of needs, thus going up one more level.

It is important to remember that the new framework, based on needs, must be built on positive qualities, resources and positive reinterpretations of behaviors, motives and goals. Only then the patient will have a positive and natural motivation towards change of the old pattern.

Reframing of the old behaviors in a new framework

Reframing the old behaviors into the new framework means generally putting together all that was previously done and summarizing it in the form of a new pattern of behavior. In the process of Structural Pattern Reframing, the patient displays and talks about many behaviors connected with the old pattern of behavior. Now, that the therapist established the new frame of reference for the behavior, he or she needs to put the behavior into this framework. In general, it means one is to collect all the reframing and reinterpretation that was done on the previous stages and put it all together into the new framework. In this new framework all the behaviors are supposed to be reframed and reoriented around the needs the therapist and patient identified. All the behaviors are supposed to grow up from the needs, for instance the need for love, support, connection, and so on. In consequence, all the needs should be reframed in a positive way, as ways of satisfying a positive need. In such a way, new sets of behavior are supposed to be introduced.

Expanding the new pattern of behavior

Expanding the new pattern of behavior is a very important part of the fourth stage of the intervention. The old habits and ways of thinking are usually very well trained and mastered. When the therapist works with a patient, he or she usually focuses only on a very small part of the whole problem reality. What we analyze and change during the session or sessions are a single samples of the behavioral pattern. From the chapter dedicated to the general concept of a pattern of behavior we know that a pattern may be a broad concept. It can function and manifest itself on many levels of communication and functioning. It may also be in conjunction and correlation with some other pattern in the general context. One can say that the pattern may be interrelated with different patterns within the system, a family system, marital system, or friendship system, or any other that involves more than one person in a relation of some sort.

If the therapist helped the patient change just this small piece of behavior he brought to the session, there would be a great possibility that the results would be short term and would not persist. Think for a moment about our jealous patient, and generally about many patients who live somewhere, in a place with other members of the household. Now, think about the system in which one person acts in a certain way, for example, with jealousy and aggression. It is almost certain that all the other people also developed their pattern to deal with the behavior of the patient. The pattern therapist is observing during the session may also be a result of some other member's pattern of behavior, it may be a response pattern. The therapist may be doing all what they can think of, and they may create a great change in the behavior, but in a long term it may all be discarded or diminished by the outside reality. In general, after the session, a patient always goes back to their reality and functions in there. The old pattern of behavior is dysfunctional but, in a way, dealing with the reality around. After the session, the patient goes back to this reality, the unchanged reality. Even if the change is real and observable, many times the surrounding does not support or does not believe in the change. The close ones know the person very well, and they all know that they behaved in some way all their lives. They just do not believe in a change. On some other occasions, the patterns of other people around the patient are so well learned and were used for such a long time that it is very difficult to break them, and these patterns are indirectly also supporting the pattern of the patient. Therefore, it is very important to expand the new interpretation of the behavior onto other members of the system that could support in some way the old patterns, either with lack of support or by their own well oiled patterns. It is important to prepare a person for that kind of situations where lack of support and some other things may occur.

The therapist may do it by expanding the new interpretation of the pattern onto the family members. It is almost certain that, for example, a husband developed a counter pattern to the one that the wife created. If the wife reacted with aggression on situations where her husband was going out with friends, the husband, for example, could develop a pattern of withdrawal. Once, the author had in therapy such a couple, when the wife developed the pattern of aggression towards the husband every time he wanted to go somewhere with friends. Through the time he started to ignore all his wife's behaviors and thus it made her even more tensed and aggressive. She felt totally ignored and frustrated. They came seeking for therapy as a last chance to do anything, before the divorce. When they entered the office they seem to the author like totally absent one to another, each in his/her own world. The main pattern to work with was the wife's pattern. She acquired it long ago in her childhood. That was an active pattern that created the passive aggressive response within the husband. To make it short, Structural Pattern Reframing model was applied for both of them. The patterns were analyzed and put into the context of the needs. It enabled them to see their own situations in different contexts. Then, the husband's pattern was presented to the wife as a response of a man who would like to do something to make her happy but is in a place where he does not know what to do. She was able to understand that when he presents such a behavior, she would have to act differently than before. The wife's pattern was presented to the husband as a display of lack of safety and need for love. Then, they were able to learn in step four how to react one on another and how to satisfy these needs in a relationship. During the session the need for meeting other people was addressed and reframed as well. It was also analyzed in a framework of the needs, so that both of them could understand more deeply the function of it. Lastly, the examples of previously displayed behaviors were discussed in the new framework, as well as the patterns in general. In such a way the new reality of the pattern was extended on the specific behaviors outside the office, the new meaning was given to such behaviors. Also, the new framework which reframed the pattern of a patient was extended to the pattern of another patient. In such a way, the whole situation can be perceived in a different, change promoting way.

Same principle of expanding the new framework for the pattern applies, when the therapist works only with one person in the family. On the first stages of the intervention, the therapist gathers the information and then works with it in such a way to provide new future interpretations and behaviors. On this stages (first three stages of the model), one also needs to gather the information about the family background, current situation and especially about other people involved in the patterns. On this stage of the intervention, the therapist changes the old way the patient perceives the behaviors and reactions of others in such a way to facilitate and support change. The therapist may first put the reactions and behaviors of the people mentioned by the patient into the categories of the patterns, and then put them into the framework of the needs. It is important so that these needs would be complementary with the patient's needs in order they could see that one pattern is a consequence of another, like in the example of the couple described above. The therapist may also meet disbelief or doubt from the family of the patient. They may reframe it in such a way, so that patient could see it as a test. A good example of such a reframing may be seen in one of Anthony Robbins interventions (Robbins & Madanes, 2005b), when he assumed that a wife may not believe in the change of the husband and that she will test if he really "is there for her". She could behave in many different unpleasant ways to see if the change is permanent, as well as because she needs a support and acceptance.

In general, it is important to incorporate the behaviors of different people into the new interpretation for a few reasons. First of all, to avoid the situation in which some behaviors in the family will take the patient from the track back to his old problem reality. Second, if such behaviors occur, to create within a patient a new way of looking at it and reacting to it - a way that would be change promoting and would facilitate the new pattern of behavior. To summarize, therapist does not change only the pattern of behavior and its meaning to the patient but also the reality of the problem and patterns of the important other ones.

In general, the change of meaning of family members reaction prevents a patient from thinking in terms:

"I changed my behavior but they don't"

or

"Everything is as it was before"

The question is, each time the same:

How can we reinterpret the behaviors of the other members of the family and friends that will not change automatically in a way to support the new interpretation and create attitude more like:

"They still do it in the old fashioned way, I wander when will they switch?"

or

"They seem to test me now more and more, so I have to show them more with my behavior what this is all about."

To achieve such an attitude one has to reframe such behaviors so that they would support the new identity. They may be changed into the trials, tests, the problems others have with change (this indicate that the person can help them in a way) an so on.

Exploration of possibilities

At this point during the treatment plan, the therapist explores with the patient new possibilities of action. The aim of this procedure is to test the new reality, test the new attitude and understanding. It is not the same as an assignment for the client.

On this stage the therapist together with the client analyze previous situations and previous actions and they try to find an answer to the question: How would You react now? What would You do now?

The purpose of this procedure is to validate if the new interpretation really works. The person may, for instance, display some of the old pattern ideas on reaction. It is important to capture this moments and do further work with it. If not well reframed and added into the new pattern of behavior, that kind of manifestations might bring the old pattern back in its place. If the patient displays the old pattern remains (an imaginative reaction to something that does not fit into the new interpretation, but rather serves the old pattern), the therapist proceeds with it similarly to working with the pattern. He asks about the consequences, leads the patient deeper into the understanding of the structure of such a choice. The therapist attaches such remains into the old pattern, showing its consequences. Then, together with the patient he searches for different solutions.

On the other hand, patient may just create many new responses and new ideas as a result of these questions. In such a case the exploration of possibilities gives them further insight into their new abilities and it also reinforces the new pattern of behavior and the new framework as a whole.

It is important on this stage to find all the remains of the old pattern by testing the new reality and reframe it, as well as to reinforce the new reality in place of the old pattern. The more remains the therapist identifies and changes on this stage, the less probable the possibility of the old pattern to reoccur in the future is.

5. Reinforcing of the new pattern of behavior and future orientation

The main purpose of this last stage of the intervention is to reinforce or empower the new pattern of behavior so that it will persist in future. The therapist is supposed to remember that the new pattern of behavior is still a new and fragile structure that is very prone to any changes and especially regression to the old well known patterns. To avoid that from happening, the therapist should provide the patient with the experiences that will enforce the new pattern and prevent it from regression processes. The following chapter presents some ways of doing it on many levels, from the cognitive and emotional level, through meaning to the pure behavioral levels.

Multi-modal positive results experience

One of the ways of creating the compelling future that would motivate the patient to maintain the new pattern of behavior and create further changes is to create a multi-modal positive results experience that would motivate the patient. Many times the old pattern of behavior creates within the patient a negative vision of the future. Aaron Beck incorporated this propriety as one of three ingredients of his cognitive triad (Beck et al., 1979). In his model, Beck names three kinds of negative thoughts that usually are coexisting with the depression. These are the negative thoughts about the self, world and future. It is important to deal with all three components during the process of treatment. The therapist deals with the negative thoughts about self and world on the earlier levels of the intervention, while creating the new framework and new patterns with the patient. At that points s/he reframes the negative things and the behavior in such a way so that it emerges from the positive intention of a kind. In this way the negative thoughts about the self decrease. By reframing the broader context of the pattern and involving the significant others into the new framework, one changes the world view into more positive. The future orientation is supposed to change a bit as a result of all this work, but a direct work on this part starts here. The patient is already familiar with the new framework and he or she is able to use it to create different future visions from those that previously derived from the old pattern.

To create such a compelling vision for the future, the therapist may use the visualization techniques. In such a visualization, the patient's aim is to see themselves in the future behaving in a new way, accordingly to the new pattern of behavior. The results of such actions end up in a positive way, rewarding the patient. These actions end up satisfying the previously unsatisfied needs and goals that were the basis for the old pattern of behavior. Previously, when the old pattern was functioning, the patient was feeling many negative emotions due to the consequences of the pattern and the fact, that the pattern did not lead to the satisfaction of the needs and goals standing behind it. Now, the patient can feel different emotions, see different results and experience a feeling of success. The experience created in such a way is supposed to be multi-modal, which means it is supposed to utilize all senses, all sensory modalities (Grinder et al., 1977), and both cognitive and emotional sides of all events in life. The more modalities the therapist is able to reach within a patient in a process of creating such a visualization, the stronger the visualization will be, and the stronger impact it will have on the patient in their future. So, in general, it is important that it has:

The visual component – the patient sees things, people, their reaction and many other things.

The vocal component – he may as well hear the joy, happiness, and many other things.

The kinesthetic component – he may feel many things, both external, like grass or sand under their feet, and internal like warmth within the body spreading or vibrating or any other internal sensation, like tensions, thrills and so on.

The cognitive component – patient may notice changes in thinking processes, how many more positive and optimistic thoughts are present when the new pattern is applied, and so on.

The emotional component – What kind of emotions accompany the vision; patient may feel joy, happiness, excitement and so on.

The therapist creates with the patient such a multi-modal vision starting from the patient themselves and their behaviors and then adding the responses and behaviors of other people, thus spreading the positive and compelling future vision. It is also important to go through many situations rather than focusing on only one. In such a way, the therapist also spreads the positive future vision. Such a vision is supposed to be defined in general terms, to permit some changes in future. It is also supposed to include some negative responses of the environment on the patient and their new behavior, all reframed in a positive, change promoting way.

Addressing of states and processes

When the compelling motivating vision of the future is created, the therapist may address the states and processes to it. Addressing is a process of dividing between the emotions and behaviors from the old pattern that the patient discarded, and the consequences and emotions derived from the new pattern. The purpose of this procedure is to enforce the connection between the old pattern and aversive emotions and the new pattern and positive ones. It has a motivational value.

In general, the therapist addresses the new positive emotions that appeared to the new pattern and all aversive to the old pattern of behavior. One can do it simply by talking about it to the patient. The therapist may ask what differences the patient can already see, and then they may also create a complete reality vision in which they simply create the causal connections between the old emotions and old pattern and new emotions with new pattern of behavior.

Freeing the non-verbal channel from the old pattern

As mentioned few times before, the pattern of behavior, no matter if old or new, will manifest itself on various levels of communication, behavior and so on. It can manifest in communication in a direct fashion, when the patient just talks about the problem. It can also manifest itself in a metaphorical way, when the patient uses the metaphors and parables in describing the problem. It can also manifest itself through behaviors and non-verbal communication. At this point of the intervention, the therapist already managed to deal with the viewpoint generated by the pattern through reframing processes. Emotional component of the pattern is also changed at this point of the intervention partly due to the change in the thinking pattern. Behavior is also supposed to change due to these changes in some part. Many times, however, when the cognitive and even emotional part of the pattern seems to be positively restructured, the non-verbal communication, as one of the unconscious components of the old pattern, is still under its influence. It basically means that sometimes we can observe some kind of non-verbal clues while talking about the pattern or displaying it. It may be some facial expression, grimace or some stereotypic movement, that accompanies the talking, thinking about or just doing the behavior from the pattern set. Many times a simple operation of pointing out this fact to a patient enables him or her to gain some more control. Sometimes when the non-verbal part is still attached to the old pattern in a form of some mimic gesture or stereotypical movement, it means that some other work is supposed to be done with the pattern because there are some remains still present. The therapist can choose to work with it in various ways. For instance, they can create a metaphor that will help a patient to pass from the old pattern to the new one. One can also work with such a gesture later on, in the end of the intervention as with any other pattern of behavior. As for now, if it is present, the therapist can assume that it is still a remain of the old pattern and may evaporate during further work. At this point they can just notate that it is there and observe what happens with it during further work.

Closing of the pattern (reframing)

When all the previous work is done, the therapist may want to close the pattern. Sometimes, when the new pattern and a new framework are established, there are still some old habits present. The closing of the pattern of behavior involves further questioning about the future reactions and thought patterns, as well as emotional reactions and any other part of the pattern of behavior. The patient, when answers these questions, may demonstrate a complete change of the pattern, and then this part serves just to enforce the new pattern reality. Sometimes, there are still some parts of the old thinking habits present in patient's answers. For example, he or she may still try to react in a dominant way or in an aggressive fashion to achieve some goals. If this occurs, such a manifestation is supposed to be treated as a pattern itself, so it is supposed to be put into the framework of needs, for example, and the consequences are supposed to be drawn out of it in such a way so that patient could see and understand how such a behavior applies to the old pattern and why it is still not well adjusted. It is important to remember that it is the patient who has to come to these conclusions with some help from the therapist. The role of the therapist is not to impose some arbitrary interpretation on the subject, but rather to guide him or her in a process of discovering and looking for answers by themselves. When the patient comes to the conclusion that the behavior still comes from the same source, the therapist may ask about how they (the patient) would react now in the same situation. In such a way, the therapist may evaluate if the change occurred. The pattern is closed when all such manifestations, if present, are reframed and changed into new pattern reactions.

New meaning creation

Another important ingredient of the positive change is the meaning attached to it. In the final step of the intervention, we not only progress the new ways of behavior into the future by a multi-level visualization. If we want the new identity, the new ways of behavior persist through time and to get through the old pattern reality and even change it, it (the new identity and ways of behavior) has to have purpose. In other words, it has to have a meaning attached to it.

The concept of meaning was in its today sense introduced by an Austrian psychiatrist Victor Frankl as a part of his new approach to therapy called the logotherapy (Frankl, 1984, 2009, 2010). According to Frankl, a man in general has to be in move. The natural state for any person in the world is to strive to something, or as he puts it, to constantly pass beyond one's own existence towards something more (Frankl, 1984, 2010). In other words, the natural state for any human being is a developmental state. Lack of such a movement, based on lack of challenges to deal with, can cause so called existential emptiness due to lack of meaning (Frankl, 2009, 2010). On the other hand, the meaning found in, even the most hopeless contexts like concentration camp or terminal illness, can help people to deal with the reality with dignity and even find the motivation to survive (Frankl, 2009). In a more causal contexts Alex Pattakos provides evidence (Pattakos, 2004, 2008), that people working, for example, in governmental services, doing monotone and many times unpleasant work, who found a meaning in their job, are able to do it much better, derive a lot satisfaction from it, and even avoid burnout in the future.

Victor Frankl (Frankl, 2009, 2010) in his conception of meaning points out few very important features of the meaning that we will now shortly address to understand more completely what the meaning is and how to work with it.

First of all, there is no such a thing as the general meaning of life or something similar. Meaning in this conception is something that every person has to find for him/her self in each and every situation separately. With the meaning, a person takes on him/herself a kind of responsibility for its realization. A person pursues a goal that is derived from the meaning.

Secondly, as mentioned above, it is the meaning which generates goals that people want to fulfill.

The third aspect of the meaning is its motivational nature. Contradictory to Freud's (Freud, 1977) libidal drives and energies, which push people towards certain ways of satisfaction, the meaning attracts people. In this way, it has a totally opposite nature compared to drives. It fires the internal and natural motivation of a person to develop and walk besides themselves towards others and towards goals.

To summarize, the meaning found in a situation helps people deal with the situation, sets future goals and motivates people to achieve these goals. In other words, the meaning secures the future orientation of a subject and is able to sustain the new pattern of behavior and the new framework in place, and even proceed it further.

From the above statements we already know that the meaning has to be individually discovered by the patient. In Structural Pattern Reframing however, the therapist has some tools to help patient in the process of meaning discovery.

One schema, that is of great value in this process, is the construct of the values. Every person builds their behaviors and patterns around some needs and goals. The identity of a person is built around some key values. Love, for example, can be perceived as a need, but also as a value. The needs of feeling secure and certain, for example, that lead to some behaviors can also be attached to the value of love and value of caring for family and others. It is important in this schema to, first of all, identify some key values that stand behind the needs that drive the behavioral patterns. When the therapist finds the key value, they may build on it, together with the patient, the meaning for the future that would incorporate the important needs and new patterns of behavior. The therapist builds the reality, in which they find together with the patient their (patient's) key values and create the meaning out of it. The meaning sets specific goals for the future. Then, the therapist attaches the new patterns and new framework to it. In other words, the ways to fulfill the goals and the meaning lead through the new patterns of behavior and the new general framework. Such a new interpretation is based on the meaning and supported by it.

Assignments

The last thing the therapist may choose to do with the patient is to create together special assignments for the future. It is important to mention that we do not mean here the assignments created in such a fashion like within the Cognitive Therapy Approach (Beck et al., 1979), like, for example, thought protocols and so on. These kind of assignments, although of great value in some cases, need to be checked and revised on the next sessions. Since in this project the analysis was performed on cases of single session treatments, the nature of the assignments are a bit different.

The main purpose of assignments discussed below are similar to main goals of posthypnotic suggestions, which are to reinforce the new framework and patterns of behavior through some experiences, or in other words, to actualize some idea later in behavior (Erickson & Rossi, 1979). In fact, since the therapist is not present after the intervention in the life of the subject (even if the course of treatment lasts for more than one session, the application of new patterns of behavior will most likely take place between sessions), we should consider giving an assignment to the subject as a form of posthypnotic suggestion.

Let us now, therefore, focus briefly on the structure of the posthypnotic suggestion, as outlined by Milton H. Erickson in his book *Hypnotherapy – an Exploratory Casebook* (Erickson & Rossi, 1979).

First of all, the therapist can attach the suggestion, or an assignment to the truisms in life of the person. A truism is something obvious that will happen, or something inevitable. This can develop a yes set, a pattern of agreement for what the therapist just says, and is more difficult to reject. For example, the therapist may put the assignment in such a context:

> *So next time You go back home, you close the door and enter the household You would ... (then follows the assignment)*

As you can see, the statements *Go back home, close the door, enter the household* are three truisms that usually happen before any communication with the other inhabitants can occur. The client usually agrees with the first three statements, and with the fourth as well, as a consequence of the yes set.

Another important thing is a surprise. One can induce the surprise by just saying:

> *I wonder how surprising will it be for You and others to see and experience yourself in this new way.*

There are two suggestions in this statement: *Experiencing yourself in a new way,* and that *it will be surprising for the patient and others.*

The element of surprise tends to suspend patients habitual set, or old framework and starts the unconscious search, according to Milton H. Erickson (Erickson & Rossi, 1979). Since in the Structural Pattern Reframing the old set was already broken, the element of surprise serves to support the new framework and new patterns derived from it.

Surprise can also be an element of an assignment. The therapist may ask a patient to act differently than previously in a specific situation, and tell them the following:

> *I wonder how surprised You will be with the outcome.*

The new emotions that will emerge and the new feeling and thought can surprise the patient. It can, therefore, evoke higher expectancies and motivation towards trying out the new ways of behavior.

Types of the assignments

Before discussing the types of the assignments, it is important to point out what the purpose of the assignment in the Structural Pattern Reframing model is. By assigning some future tasks, the therapist supports and enriches the still fresh and new representation of the new framework and pattern of behavior. The assignments may also serve as a closure for the patient in cases in which some more work has to be done. After pointing out some types of the assignments, we will discuss the role of this assignments in the process of pattern reframing.

One of the most useful classifications of the assignments for the purpose of this paper is the one provided by Stephen and Carol Lankton (C. H. Lankton, 1988; S. R. Lankton & Lankton, 1986). They name three kind of assignments in therapy: the paradoxical, skill-building, and the ambiguous function assignments.

Paradoxical Assignments

Paradoxical assignments were for the first time described by Victor Frankl (Frankl, 2009) but some of its elements can also be found in the work of many others, like for instance Adler (Weeks & L'Abate, 1982). Generally speaking, the technique of the paradox leads to obtain a different framework for, or in other words, different viewpoint on the symptomatic behavior. Many times paradoxical intervention is based on the idea to continue having the symptom, and through this, changing the frame of reference for the problem (C. H. Lankton, 1988). Many examples of the paradoxical assignments were delivered by Milton H Erickson and described especially by Jay Haley (Haley, 1973, 1985a, 1985b, 1985c), and are in detail discussed therein. One of the examples of the paradoxical intervention was described by

Milton H. Erickson within a case of a patient having phantom limb pains (Erickson & Rossi, 1979; C. H. Lankton, 1988). Generally speaking, the patient was suffering from the phantom limb pains, and Erickson suggested him that he can develop this and many other feelings in his wooden leg. He can, for example, develop a pleasant feelings in it. Of course, the process took some time to work and was gradual. One can see the detailed description in Erickson's book *Hypnotherapy an Exploratory Casebook* (Erickson & Rossi, 1979). In here we only use it to shortly demonstrate a paradoxical principle. In this case, the therapist took the symptom and developed it into something else.

The author finds paradoxical interventions very helpful, as well. Many times in family therapy, when the family members are constantly quarreling, the author advices them to set a specific time for such an important activity. The author at this point accepts the problem and encourages people to develop it in a way which change the frame of reference. But there is also another process involved in this. Since they will set specific times for a quarrel, they unconsciously gain control over the problem, and it is not so easy to quarrel when planned.

In the Structural Pattern Reframing model, the paradoxical interventions can be very helpful at the previous steps of the intervention, for instance, at time when the frame is being built and then, as a consequence, when the old pattern is being questioned and broken by the client. The paradoxical techniques can help the therapist go through both steps, due to the fact that it, when applied, changes the context of the problem and also in a way gives the symptom some different meaning making it pointless to continue in the same form. In such a way, the pattern may also be broken.

In the end of the intervention, however, such an assignments can also be useful to prevent some habitual sets to occur in the future. It is important to note, however, that many paradoxical interventions requires some additional work in the course of next sessions.

Skill-building Assignments

Skill-building assignments, also known as "homework", can be utilized when the behavioral goal is clearly specified, the client has the resources needed to build up the skill of some sort and the treatment is generally short-term (C. H. Lankton, 1988; S. R. Lankton & Lankton, 1986). Homework is most widely used in the Cognitive Approaches. Aaron Beck states, that the homework purpose has to be clearly explained to the patient (Beck et al., 1979). In other words, the therapist should provide the rationale for the procedure. Beck stresses out that in Cognitive Therapy therapist should outline the real goals and ideas standing behind the treatment plan to the patient. Carol Lankton (C. H. Lankton, 1988), however, claims that on some occasions, that kind of knowledge can be counterproductive and can produce resistant responses.

In the Structural Pattern Reframing we do not define which approach is better, it probably depends on a client. There will be clients that will work better in a rationale framework of the CBT and some other ones will resist to some aspects of it. The author, however, at many occasions works with the clients in a paradoxical way, and does not expose real goals standing behind the treatment. Both Beck and Lankton, however agree, that some explanation has to be given to the patient. Carol Lankton (C. H. Lankton, 1988), for instance, provides us with the example of the woman in therapy who was asked by the therapist for a favor to go to the nursing home to talk to one of the patients. The real goal was to develop the social skills of the patient, and formally the therapist asked only for a favor. With this procedure the therapist avoids possible resistance towards direct procedures of developing the skills the patient had problems with.

Also such indirect skill-building assignments were given by Anthony Robbins at the end stage of his interventions. For example, in the case of Lisa (Robbins & Madanes, 2004b), previously mentioned few times in this book. Lisa was an old lady who, due to her family background, had to behave more like a man than a woman. In other words, her femininity was suppressed. In the final step of the intervention, Anthony Robbins gave her few assignments, and one of these assignments was to go shopping with a friend and buy some purses. It was an indirect way of developing her femininity due to the fact that this is a very feminine thing to do.

During the process of creation of such an assignment, the therapist is supposed to remember that it has to be very specific, at best attached to specific activity, place and time, and the activity has to be very specific (Beck et al., 1979; C. H. Lankton, 1988; S. R. Lankton & Lankton, 1986). The assignment has to be so well defined to avoid rejection. It is more difficult to reject something very specific than something general in case of assignments. A general assignments may not include enough information to be properly done by the patient. The purpose of assigning the specific activity is so that it would be more difficult for the patient not to do it. It is easier to learn a complicated task step by step than all at once (Beck et al., 1979). As an example, take a case study presented by Aaron Beck (Beck et al., 1979). The subject of the therapy was a depressed woman. The therapist identified an activity that was giving her a lot of pleasure prior to the depression period. Now, however, she clams, she is unable to read, to focus attention and so on. The therapist, at the therapeutic session, gave her a very short story to read, and told her to just start to read the first paragraph, maybe the first word, then the first sentence and then the paragraph. She did all these assignments. As a result she read the whole page, and in a week was able to read a book. Her state was very much improved.

The last important feature of the skill building assignment is that it is supposed to start in the office, with the therapist (Beck et al., 1979). Many times it is difficult for the client to start the activity for him or herself. It may be due to the particular problem like depression, for instance, or some kind of negative attitude. That is why it is important to start the process at the office where the patient will be forced to attend the activity and will feel the results. That kind of positive change may reinforce the new way of behavior and give the patient at least some motivation to persist. Once again, it is important to stress out that the assignment is not supposed to be something huge and complicated. Such a complete change will certainly be rejected because it seems like a lot of work and the patient will most likely perceive it as impossible to be done. Notice that in the example above, the therapist started with one word, and then proceeded to the paragraph, the rest was done by the patient herself and by the internal processes that launched during the initial intervention.

Ambiguous Function Assignments

Ambiguous function assignments are a kind of tasks given to the patient that are highly specific and unusual themselves. Many times the task is formally irrelevant in any way to the problem, and the goal or reason for it stays unknown to the patient (C. H.

Lankton, 1988). That kind of assignments purpose is to provoke deeper processes of inner search on the unconscious level to occur. The outcome of such an assignment is usually much more than the therapist could predict in the beginning. Carol Lankton (C. H. Lankton, 1988) provides us with good examples of such assignments. For example, Erickson would, from time to time, send some of his patients to climb Squaw Peak to find there something or just to climb the mountain without giving any reason for it. Sometimes the purpose was to test someone motivation towards therapy, on a different occasion he sent someone there to outline to him or her some of his/her problem behavior. For more examples one can go directly to Carol Lankton paper (C. H. Lankton, 1988), or to the following literature for some more examples (Haley, 1973, 1985a, 1985b, 1985c).

Ambiguous function assignment (C. H. Lankton, 1988), to be properly tailored to the patient, is supposed to happen in their broader context, in their own environment. That kind of assignment is supposed to involve the patient in an active way. The patient is supposed to do something, usually with some physical object.

Another important thing to remember is what to do when the patient comes next time to the office. There are many options of what could happen. For example, the patient can do the assignment, and bring some ideas and questions with them, they may also do the assignment to some extend but not all of it, and finally they might not have done the assignment at all. It is important to utilize any response given towards supporting the therapeutic change or a goal. In other words, the therapist is supposed to reframe the whole situation in such a way so that it would, no matter what the result is, support the therapeutic goal and prove something new to the patient.

That type of assignment is more accurate and suitable for the multisession treatment in which the therapist can work further with the outcome of such an assignment. In the context of the Structural Pattern Reframing model, where someone decides to use it as a single session model, the therapist must use such assignments with a lot of care and caution in order not to leave the patient with some process open and unfinished. It is, however, still possible to gain huge benefits from that kind of assignments when the patient is properly motivated. The process standing behind it is, however, different than with other assignments. Its purpose is not to empower the new pattern of behavior, but to let the patient decide on the meaning. In other words, the patient's homework is here to fulfill the ambiguous situation with the meaning. It is important, therefore, to create assignments in such a way so that the new framework would be more preferred in assigning a meaning to the activity.

Structural Assignments – the summary

In the Structural Pattern Reframing model the therapist may decide to utilize all of the above processes. As previously said, some of the assignments, like for example paradoxical one, and an ambiguous function assignments are more suitable for multisession treatment, or can be better used on the earlier stages of the intervention to decompose the old framework. Paradoxical assignments have huge potential for breaking the pattern in an indirect way. The therapist may gradually create a new framework that will enable the patient in the end to question the usefulness of a certain pattern of behavior, or they may design the paradoxical intervention to change the meaning of the symptom and cause its disappearance. In the end of the intervention in the Structural Pattern Reframing model it is advised to the therapist to use mostly the skill – building assignments to stimulate further development of the new pattern of behavior.

To make it all even clearer, let us look at all the three types of assignments for the point of view of what they are focused on. The paradoxical assignment focuses on the old pattern of behavior, therefore, it is advised to use it on the earlier stages of the intervention when the therapist still works with the old pattern and there is a possibility to question it indirectly. There is one exception from this rule, however. The paradoxical assignment can be given in the end if we want to give the patient some tool to gain control over the unconscious symptom by doing something new with it. Like in the case of the patient with the phantom limb pain, they may develop the pain into many other forms of feelings after the intervention, as well. In conclusion, such assignments enable patient to experience the problem in a new way, without previous work with perspective and may be most useful on the third stage, when the pattern is supposed to be broken.

The ambiguous function assignments are undefined in their nature. These are very useful if we want to provide a patient with the new understandings for the situation. It is, therefore, also advised to use them on the earlier stages of the intervention, where the therapist may control and eventually reframe the outcome. These assignments may, however, be also used in the end stage if the patient has a new framework well developed and will frame the experience in a new way.

The skill-building assignment is, however, oriented towards the future goals and may with great benefit support the new framework by specific actions that will directly or indirectly utilize the new ways of reacting and behaving.

These criteria clearly show how we can use and utilize various kinds of assignment and why it is better to use some type over the other in a particular case on the particular step of the intervention.

How to use the model?

In this final part of the book we will shortly address some key aspects of general application of the Structural Pattern Reframing Model. We will try to answer the question of what it is and how to work with it to achieve the best possible results.

What is this model really?

The reader, while reading this book, is supposed to keep in mind that the model presented in this book is not an actual paradigm of psychotherapy or coaching. It is a summarized result of six years of research and observations. Even though it is based on the work of Milton H. Erickson, Anthony Robbins and Byron Katie, it does not describe the way these people work. The model shows the key points all these three people share in some part together and thus reflects the style of work of neither of them. It rather shows us an idea of work, something that is otherwise unnoticeable. The general model of work is based on these three examples.

One session treatment – multisession approach

Another important feature, as well as limitation of the model, is that it was based on one session treatments. Due to this fact, the model limits number of techniques and ideas to such ones that could be utilized during one session treatment. That is the reason why, for instance, it is advised to use skill-building assignments rather than, for example, paradoxical or ambiguous-function ones. The last two usually require some feedback. This, however, does not mean that these are less valuable if we assume a multisession model for treatment.

Despite this limitation the model can be used in a multisession treatment in two ways.

Firstly, we can use the whole general model to focus on a certain problem during single session, and then work with its remains on the next one. That may go on until the whole problem is solved. It is also advised to do it in the situation when there is a risk that the problem is complicated and multileveled. It means that many symptoms are interrelated and the problem manifests on many levels. In such a case, we may deal with separate aspects one by one, uncovering the deeper causes.

The second way, if we deal with a problem that needs more session, is to divide the models steps into sessions. In this instance, we can close the first step after one or two session and then another, till the last one. In such a case, the therapist must use their intuition and observable indicators described in this book to be able to judge when it is the time for another step to occur.

Always follow the patient

One has to remember that it is the patient who knows best about their lives, their problems and what is best for them, even if they do not know it yet on a conscious level. Due to this reason, it is the patient to decide when it is the time to go on another level of the intervention. We only observe and if we can see the acceptance of the ingredients required to attend another level, then we can try to do it. In the processes such as reframing, pattern breaking or, for instance, meaning creation it is the patient who does the work. The therapist only creates the supporting climate for a change and accompanies the patient in the process of change. As a companion, they may interest patient with some new ideas, may suggest the course from time to time, but never drag or pull the patient into any place.

The indirect ways to alter the pattern of behavior
The model of therapy presented in this book operates on multilevel processes of perspective shifting, reframing and meaning change. This gives us a wide variety of implementation possibilities. There are, however, such cases in which additional indirect work should be done in order to achieve complete recovery from symptoms. When the symptom set is in nature unconscious, automatic and out of patient's conscious range of influence (for instance in case of some forms of auto-aggressive, obsessive-compulsive, very deep depressive forms of behavior) the Structural Pattern Reframing model needs to be supplemented with techniques of symptom reformulation on unconscious level.

Such techniques in particular will be discussed in the second volume dedicated especially to the patterns of work of Milton H. Erickson, and will create a complete set with this book.

References

American Psychiatric Association. (1994). *Diagnostic and Statistical Manual of Mental Disorders, Fourth Edition.* Washington D. C.: American Psychiatric Association.

Andreas, C., & Andreas, S. (1989). *Heart of the Mind - engaging your inner power to change with Neurolinguistic Programming.* Boulder: Real People Press.

Bandler, R. (1992). *Magic in Action.* Capitola, CA: Meta Publications Inc.

Bandler, R., & Grinder, J. (1975). *The Structure of Magic Vol. 1 – A Book about Language and Therapy.* Palo Alto, California: Science and Behavior Books Inc.

Bandler, R., & Grinder, J. (1982). *Reframing, Neuro-Linguistic Programming and the Transformation of Meaning.* Moab, Utah: Real People Press.

Bandler, R., & MacDonald, W. (1988). *Insider's Guide to Submodalities.* Capitola, CA: Meta Publications Inc.

Beck, A. T., Garry Emery, & Ruth L. Greenberg. (1985). *Anxiety disorders and phobias: A cognitive perspective.* New York: Basic Books.

Beck, A. T., Rush, A. J., Shaw, B. F., & Emery, G. (1979). *Cognitive Therapy of Depression.* New York: The Guilford Press.

Bem, S., L. (2000). *Męskość - kobiecość: O różnicach wynikających z płci.* Gdańsk: Gdańskie Wydawnictwo Psychologiczne.

Byron, K. (2008). *Who Would You Be Without Your Story?* (C. Williams, Ed.). California: Hay House, Inc.

Byron, K. (2013). *"My mother is irresponsible with her health"* The Work of Byron Katie. Retrieved from http://www.youtube.com/watch?v=hS9ndjVjKt0&list=UU8dv ufocK9zM6KnkronGbzA

Einstein, A. (2001). O teorii względności. In *Pisma Filozoficzne* (pp. 90–93). Warszawa: De Agostini Polska Sp. z o. o.

Erickson, M. H. (1980a). A Therapeutic Double Bind Utilizing Resistance. In E. L. Rossi (Ed.), *Innovative Hypnotherapy - The Collected Papers of Milton H. Erickson on Hypnosis Volume IV* (pp. 229–232). New York: Irvington Publishers, Inc.

Erickson, M. H. (1980b). Further experimental investigation of hypnosis: Hypnotic and nonhypnotic realities. In E. L. Rossi (Ed.), *The Nature of Hypnosis and Suggestion - The Collected Papers of Milton H. Erickson on Hypnosis Volume I* (pp. 18–82). New York: Irvington Publishers, Inc.

Erickson, M. H. (1980c). Futher Clinical Techniques of Hypnosis: Utilization Techniques. In E. L. Rossi (Ed.), *The Nature of Hypnosis and Suggestion - The Collected Papers of Milton H. Erickson on Hypnosis Volume I* (pp. 177–205). New York: Irvington Publishers, Inc.

Erickson, M. H. (1980d). Hypnosis in Obstetrics: Utilizing Experiential Learnings. In E. L. Rossi (Ed.), *Innovative Hypnotherapy - The Collected Papers of Milton H. Erickson on Hypnosis Volume IV*. New York: Irvington Publishers, Inc.

Erickson, M. H. (1980e). Initial experiments investigating the nature of hypnosis. In E. L. Rossi (Ed.), *The Nature of Hypnosis and Suggestion - The Collected Papers of Milton H. Erickson on Hypnosis Volume I* (pp. 3–17). New York: Irvington Publishers, Inc.

Erickson, M. H. (1980f). Migraine Headache in a Resistant Patient. In E. L. Rossi (Ed.), *Innovative Hypnotherapy - The Collected Papers of Milton H. Erickson on Hypnosis Volume IV*. New York: Irvington Publishers, Inc.

Erickson, M. H., & Rossi, E. L. (1979). *Hypnotherapy, An Exploratory Casebook*. New York: Irvington Publishers, Inc.

Erickson, M. H., Rossi, E. L., & Rossi, S. I. (1976). *Hypnotic Realities - The Induction of Clinical Hypnosis and Forms of Indirect Suggestion*. New York: Irvington Publishers, Inc.

Fenichel, O. (1954). Brief Psychotherapy. In H. Fenichel & D. Rapaport (Eds.), *The Collected Papers of Otto Fenichel* (pp. 243–259). New York: Norton.

Frankl, V. (1984). *Homo Patiens. Logoterapia i jej kliniczne zastosowanie. Pluralizm nauk a jedność człowieka. Człowiek wolny*. Warszawa: Instytut Wydawniczy PAX.

Frankl, V. (2009). *Człowiek w poszukiwaniu sensu*. Warszawa: Wydawnictwo Czarna Owca.

Frankl, V. (2010). *Wola sensu - założenia i zastosowanie logoterapii*. Warszawa: Wydawnictwo Czarna Owca.

Freud, S. (1937). *The interpretation of dreams*. New York: G. Allen & Unwin.

Freud, S. (1977). *Introductory Lectures on Psycho-analysis*. New York: W W Norton & Company Incorporated.

Goffman, E. (2006). *Rytuał Interakcyjny*. Warszawa: Wydawnictwo Naukowe PWN.

Greenwald, A. G. (1980). The Totalitarian Ego: Fabrication and Revision of Personal History. *American Psychologist*, (35), 603–618.

Grinder, J., DeLozier, J., & Bandler, R. (1977). *Patterns of the Hypnotic Techniques of Milton H. Erickson, M. D. - Volume 2.* Cupertino, CA: Meta Publications Inc.

Groesbeck, C. J. (1985). The archetypal image of the wounded healer. *Journal of Analytic Psychology*, (20), 122–127.

Haley, J. (1973). *Uncommon Therapy: The Psychiatric Techniques of Milton H. Erickson, M.D.* New York: Norton.

Haley, J. (1985a). *Conversations with Milton H. Erickson, M.D. - Volume I - Changing the Individuals.* New York: Triangle Press.

Haley, J. (1985b). *Conversations with Milton H. Erickson, M.D. - Volume II - Changing Couples.* New York: Triangle Press.

Haley, J. (1985c). *Conversations with Milton H. Erickson, M.D. - Volume III - Changing Children and Families.* New York: Triangle Press.

Howard, K. I., Lueger, R. J., Maling, M. S., & Martinovich, Z. (1993). A Phase Model of Psychotherapy Outcome: Causal Mediation of Change. *Journal of Consulting and Clinical Psychology*, 61(4), 678–685.

James, T., Flores, L., & Schober, J. (2006). *Hypnosis - A Comprehensive Guide Producing Deep Trance Phenomena.* Norwalk, CT: Crown House Publishing Company.

Lankton, C. H. (1985). Elements of an Ericksonian Approach. In S. R. Lankton (Ed.), *Elements and Dimensions of an Ericksonian Approach* (pp. 61–75). New York: Brunner/Mazel Publishers.

Lankton, C. H. (1988). Task Assignments: Logical and Otherwise. In J. K. Zeig & S. R. Lankton (Eds.), *Developing Ericksonian Therapy - State of the Art* (pp. 257–279). New York: Brunner/Mazel Publishers.

Lankton, S. R., & Lankton, C. H. (1983). *The Answer Within: A Clinical Framework of Ericksonian Hypnotherapy.* New York: Brunner/Mazel Publishers.

Lankton, S. R., & Lankton, C. H. (1986). *Enchantment and Intervention in Family Therapy - Training in Ericksonian Approaches.* New York: Brunner/Mazel Publishers.

Loftus, E. L. (1993). The Reality of Repressed Memories. *American Psychologist,* (48), 518–537.

Maslov, A. H. (1943). A theory of human motivation. *Psychological Review,* 50(4), 370–396.

Maslov, A. H. (2009). *Motywacja i Osobowość.* Warszawa: Wydawnictwo Naukowe PWN.

Maxie C Maultsby. (1984). *Rational behavior therapy.* New Jersey: Prentice-Hall.

McCraty, R., Atkinson, M., & Tomasino, D. (2001). *Science of the Heart - Exploring the Role of the Heart in Human Performance.* Boulder Creek, CA: Institute of HeartMath.

McCraty, R., Atkinson, M., Tomasino, D., & Bradley, R. T. (2006). *The Coherent Heart - Heart-Brain Interactions, Psychophisiological Coherence, and the Emergence of System-Wide Order.* Boulder Creek, CA: Institute of HeartMath.

Messer, S. B. (2002). A Psychodynamic Perspective on Resistance in Psychotherapy: Vive la Resistance. *Psychotherapy in Practice,* 58(2), 157–163.

Mills, J. C., & Crowley, R. J. (1986). *Therapeutic Metaphors for Childern and the Child Within*. New York and London: Routledge Taylor and Francis Group.

O'Hanlon, W. H. (1990). A Grand Unified Theory for Brief Therapy: Putting Problems in Context. In J. K. Zeig & S. G. Gilligan (Eds.), *Brief Therapy – Myths, Methods, and Metaphors* (pp. 78–89). New York: Brunner/Mazel Publishers.

Pattakos, A. (2004). The Search for a Meaning in Government Service. *Public Administration Review, 64*(1), 106–112.

Pattakos, A. (2008). *Prisoners of Our Thoughts - Victor Frankl's Principles for Discovering Meaning in Life and Work*. San Francisco: Berrett-Koehler Publishers, Inc.

Robbins, A. (2007). *Why we do what we do*. TED Talk. Retrieved from http://www.youtube.com/watch?v=Cpc-t-Uwv1I

Robbins, A., & Madanes, C. (2004a). *Conquering Overwhelming Loss: Rediscovering a Compelling Future*. Robbins Research International Inc.

Robbins, A., & Madanes, C. (2004b). *Reclaming Your True Identity: The Power of Vulnerability*. Robbins Research International Inc.

Robbins, A., & Madanes, C. (2005a). *Back from the Edge: Creating Everlasting Love*. Robbins Research International Inc.

Robbins, A., & Madanes, C. (2005b). *Relationship Storms: Man Enough to Stay the Course*. Robbins Research International Inc.

Rossi, E. L. (1972). *Dreams and the growth of personality: Expanding awareness in psychotherapy*. New York: Pergamon.

Rossi, E. L. (1995). *Hipnoterapia - Psychologiczne Mechanizmy Uzdrawiania*. Poznań: Zysk i S-ka Wydawnictwo.

Rossi, E. L., & Rossi, K. L. (2008). *The New Neuroscience of Psychotherapy, Therapeutic Hypnosis and Rehabilitation: A Creative Dialogue our Genes.* Los Osos, CA: Ernest Lawrence Rossi, Ph.D. and Kathryn Lane Rossi, Ph.D.

Seligman, M. E. P. (2010). *Optymizmu można się nauczyć - Jak zmienić swoje myślenie i swoje życie.* Poznań: Media Rodzina.

Skinner, B., Frederic. (1976). *About Behaviorism.* New York: Vintage Book Edition.

Walters, C., & Havens, R. A. (1994). Good News for a Change: Optimism, Altruism, and Hardiness as the Basis for Erickson's Approach. In J. K. Zeig (Ed.), *Ericksonian Methods, The Essence of the Story* (pp. 163–181). New York: Brunner/Mazel Publishers.

Watson, J. B. (1919). *Psychology from the standpoint of a behaviorist.* Philadelphia: J.B. Lippincott.

Watson, J. B. (1930). *Behaviorism.* Chicago: University of Chicago Press.

Watzlawick, P. (1978). *The Language of Chnage - Elements of Therapeutic Communication.* New York: Norton.

Watzlawick, P. (1990). Therapy Is What You Say It Is. In J. K. Zeig & S. G. Gilligan (Eds.), *Brief Therapy – Myths, Methods, and Metaphors* (pp. 55–61). New York: Brunner/Mazel Publishers.

Watzlawick, P., Weakland, J. H., & Fish, R. (1974). *Change: Principles of Problem Formulation and Problem Resolution.* New York: Norton.

Weeks, G. R., & L'Abate, L. (1982). *Paradoxical Psychotherapy: Theory and Practice with Individuals, Couples and Families.* New York: Brunner/Mazel Publishers.

Weiner, B. (1992). *Human Motivation: Metaphors, Theories, and Research*. Newbury Park, California: Sage Publications.

Whorf, B. L. (1956). The Relation of Habitual Thought and Behavior to Language. In J. B. Carroll (Ed.), *Language, Thought and Reality: Selected Writings of Benjamin Lee Whorf* (pp. 134–159). Cambridge: MIT Press.

Yapko, M. (2002). *Kiedy Życie Boli - Zalecenia w leczeniu depresji*. Gdańsk: Gdańskie Wydawnictwo Psychologiczne.

Zeig, J. K. (1980a). Sympton Prescription for Expanding the Psychotic's World View. In E. L. Rossi (Ed.), *Innovative Hypnotherapy - The Collected Papers of Milton H. Erickson on Hypnosis Volume IV* (pp. 335–337). New York: Irvington Publishers, Inc.

Zeig, J. K. (1980b). *Teaching Seminar with Milton H. Erickson*. New York: Brunner/Mazel Publishers.

Zeig, J. K. (1990). Seeding. In J. K. Zeig & S. G. Gilligan (Eds.), *Brief Therapy - Myths, Metods, and Metaphors* (pp. 221–246). New York: Brunner/Mazel Publishers.

Zeig, J. K. (1994). Advanced Techniques of Utilization: An Intervention Metamodel and the Use of Sequences, Symptom Words, and Figures of Speach. In J. K. Zeig (Ed.), *Ericksonian Methods, The Essence of the Story* (pp. 295–314). New York: Brunner/Mazel Publishers.

ABOUT THE AUTHOR

Jan Dyba is a psychologist, sociologist and psychotherapist. He runs a private psychological practice in Poland, where he works with patients utilizing ericksonian approaches to therapy. He conducts research projects aiming to search for effective ways of doing psychotherapy and facilitating interpersonal change within a person. He is a founder of NeuroTwine Research Project dedicated to scientific investigation of the outstanding psychotherapeutic performance and change processes.

www.ingramcontent.com/pod-product-compliance
Lightning Source LLC
Chambersburg PA
CBHW020508290526
45786CB00002B/528

* 9 7 8 1 5 0 0 3 6 7 8 6 2 *